Pitch Decks for Founders

By

John Biggs

Table of Contents

Foreword

For Founders books are concise, readable guides on technical topics designed for busy founders. The goal is to offer you a way to make quick decisions and learn important skills for your journey as a founder.

In this book, we'll talk about pitching. We'll explore the process of building a deck, creating a pitch, and delivering your pitch to investors or other business partners. This book is for absolute beginners but it does assume some familiarity with tools like PowerPoint and Google Docs. Further, you have to have the confidence and desire to pitch your own idea to a group of people who may or may not understand or appreciate it. That's the hardest skill to learn and the most important.

Your guide, John Biggs, has heard and given thousands of pitches during his career and his work has raised millions of dollars for various startups. He is a 15-year veteran of TechCrunch and an entrepreneur who has built and funded six successful startups.

Introduction

"Send me your deck."

Every founder has heard this request and, if you're not prepared, the result has often been fear and confusion. What's a deck? Is it a presentation? A document? A business plan?

What should go in your deck? How should you write it? Who should write it? What does a modern deck look like?

And then there are all of the ancillary questions: How do I present it? Who should present it? And what if I send it out and someone steals my idea?

Don't worry. Everything will be explained in this short book. Our goal is to make you a pitching superstar by offering you two types of pitch decks and some advice on how to give the best pitches on the block.

Pitching is about sales. The goal is to sell a product and that product, at the end of the day, is you and your company. Our goal is to teach you, an entrepreneur and founder, how to pitch confidently and sell your audience on your idea.

Pitching is a game. The goal of the game is to convince someone with money or time or talent to join you in your cause. In fact, the end goal of pitching isn't always an investment. Most pitches end without any checks or contracts signed. A pitch is often the first step in a long process but, with a good pitch, at least that process has a chance to start. In other words, the founder's journey begins with a single pitch.

Pitching is an art. Even if you're good at public speaking,

even if you have the confidence of a superhero, and even if you've pitched a million times before, every pitch is unique. Performing a good pitch is akin to performing a monologue on stage, albeit with higher states. Here's another interesting fact: as a founder, there is a very good chance that you won't be the best person to pitch your idea. Because founders are wrapped up in their projects, their dreams, and ambitions, pitches become some kind of bloodsport. The result is an uneven, overly confident mash of buzzwords and fear. Not everyone has the talent to pitch even if that talent is simply getting out of your own way and explaining your product in a few simple words.

Our advice? Use the tools we offer in this book to build a great deck and pitch. Practice your pitch as much as you can. Pitch as much as you can. And have confidence that once you master the tools we show you in this book you'll be the best pitcher in the ballpark.

What You Will Learn

In this book you will learn how to build a one-page deck, a ten-page deck, and how to pitch both types of decks comfortably in a startup environment. Decks come in all shapes and sizes, just like businesses. Maybe you're trying to raise money for an app or a hot dog cart. The techniques are the same. Our goal in this book is to teach you how to pitch a startup, a company identified as a small business with a global audience. Does this mean you can't use this book to pitch your food truck or retail shop idea to an investor? Absolutely not. It just means that we will use language and examples focused on tech startups but everything they can do you can do (better?).

This book is partially based on a version of a longer book called Get Funded! by myself, John Biggs, and my co-author Eric Villines. My goal was to make this only about pitching but if you want an in-depth look at getting funding from multiple sources, please check it out.

Use this book as an outline for your pitch preparation. Whether you're getting up in front of a roomful of investors at a big event or you're facing down one person in a tiny conference room, the tools you find here will be useful.

A pitch is a way to tell your story and can be used to tell your story when you aren't in the room. It is both a script and a self-contained tool that performs the pitch for you. In other words, it augments your story and can tell it in your stead.

Summary

When you are done reading this book you will be able to:

1. Build your own one-page deck (one-pager).

2. Build your own 10-page deck.

3. Create a "long" deck with appendices.

4. Comfortably pitch both your one-page deck and your 10-page deck.

5. Run a pitch meeting with a potential investor.

The Basics

A traditional pitch deck is usually a ten-slide PowerPoint or Keynote file that describes your startup to investors and assists you in making a case for your company. The keywords in this definition are "startup" and "investor." This book is not about general business presentations. Instead, this book offers targeted advice for anyone trying to communicate something simply to a potentially unmotivated and even hostile audience.

In this book, we will also explore the single-page or one-page deck, a tool that is often more popular than traditional 10-page decks. This type of deck is perfect for situations when an investor wants a top-down view of your product and believes they don't have the time or inclination to explore it in depth.

Think of your pitch deck as a cheat sheet for yourself and your investors. It is a standalone document - you'll often send it without being able to explain it - so it has to be completely self-contained and understandable at a very high level.

Pitch decks aren't books or manifestoes. The current writing style in pitch decks assumes no more than ten slides and less than 100 words per slide. Do not confuse a pitch deck with a one-pager or a business plan. A one-pager, which we will describe later, is a useful tool for approaching busy investors, and a business plan, while important, should not be outlined like a pitch deck.

There is often confusion when a "corporate" veteran begins to pitch for startups. This is natural. The pitch deck is, in short, a life-or-death product that can make or break your efforts. A corporate deck is a way to convince stakeholders to go along with an idea in a safe setting. They are not the same.

Decks must be as simple as possible. They might be read on a small phone in the back of an Uber or they might surface randomly during a discussion with fellow investor. Your deck will float like a feather in the wind. If that sounds poetic, please take it literally: you will have no control over who sees or does not see your deck. Prepare accordingly.

You cannot assume any level of technical understanding or patience in your audience. You also should not put anything "secret" into your deck including computer code, descriptions of patentable processes, or even photos of your product at any stage of development if (and only if) those parts aren't already public. The deck could end up anywhere - in an investor's mailbox or on a competitor's desk - so everything in the deck you need to be willing to share with the world. That said, you cannot hide the best parts of your product. If you are producing an app, include screenshots. If you're building hardware, include renders. If you're starting a hot dog truck you need to show off your frankfurters.

Your deck is an advertisement. It's a way to share your idea in a compact and very readable way and it is used to simultaneously explain your idea to a stranger who has no contact with you and to guide a conversation about your startup during a pitch meeting.

Let's talk about the different ways you'll use a pitch deck as a founder and why it's important to create the best one you can given your budget. First, let's explore why we pitch and what a pitch is - and isn't.

Your Pitch Deck Is a Business Card

Your Pitch Deck is a way to explain your company to a person who doesn't know anything about it. Therefore it should be easily accessible, be nicely laid out, and well-designed. You should always hire a professional designer to create your deck for you or, barring that, have the best "hipster" on staff design something that matches your company's design and aesthetic. You should also share your pitch deck on a service like DocSend or even Dropbox. You'll want a simple way to send people to your deck at any time. Create a simple URL - www.yourcompany.com/deck - that will forward people to your deck instantly. Alternatively, create a bit.ly link that you can pass out at a moment's notice. Like your business card, your deck should be instantly accessible.

You should control who sees your deck - within reason. Like your business card, you can decide who gets your deck. When creating a public link on your website you should, at the very least, ask for the email address of the viewer. DocSend, shown below, offers this feature and it's a great way to keep tabs on who has seen your pitch deck. Simply select "Require email to view" in order to collect the email addresses of folks who are checking out your deck.

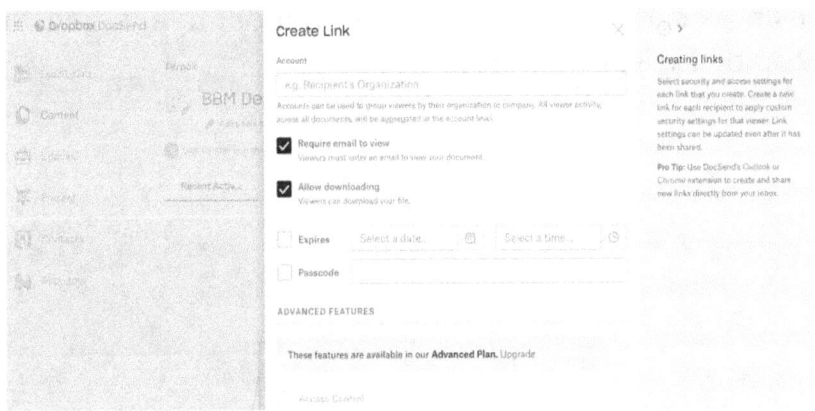

Your deck should be self-contained. Your business card doesn't contain any extraneous data. You don't include your shoe size or blood type. It should explain, at a high level, what your company does. It also introduces your team and creates a point of social proof for your product. Social proof is a concept that can basically be equated with "clout." By showing off a good, well-designed deck with a great team you add a little bit more respectability to your project.

Here's the trick, though: the opposite is also true. A poorly designed deck is a death knell for a startup. Many startup founders ignore deck design and appearance at their peril. Many of them are familiar with so-called corporate decks and assume they are sufficient. They are not. You need to put time and resources - preferably by hiring a designer - into your deck.

Don't add lawyer-required proprietary information warnings and disclaimers. Outside of the corporate world, there is no reason to clutter your deck with legalese or disclaimers (unless, of course, you're working on a financial startup). Again, this is your business card. You will be passing it out to hundreds of people… if you're lucky.

Your Pitch Deck Is a Way to Raise Money

For a venture capitalist or investor, a pitch deck is a type of shorthand. They use it in many ways.

The pitch deck is a gatekeeping mechanism. If they ask for a deck and you don't have one, they're off the hook. Also if you send a deck "later" - a week later, for example - you are immediately suspect. The deck is a way to separate those serious about funding from those who aren't. Any startup founded in the last 20 years has a pitch deck ready at all times. If an investor asks for a deck and you don't have it immediately available either via a link or PDF then you're probably not serious about raising VC capital. Any little thing can turn a "Maybe" into a "No" and there is no need to encourage the VC to turn you down.

The pitch deck makes it easy to say "no." By skimming your deck, a VC can easily decide if your company fits its investment plan. This doesn't sound great if you're trying to raise a round but it definitely helps you "fire and forget" your deck to various VCs and get quick answers. But here's the other side of that coin: never give the investor ammunition to reject you outright. As we mentioned before, a well-crafted pitch deck is an invitation to say "yes." A poorly crafted one is an invitation to pass immediately.

Most VCs have seen hundreds of startups and, more importantly, may have seen startups in the same industry. If they have not already invested in your particular area of expertise then you can convince them to invest in you by framing the problem more carefully or understanding the pain points for your customers more precisely. This should come out in your pitch deck as you describe your expertise and value to the team.

Your Pitch Deck is Your Script

When you are sitting in front of an investor, you'll need your deck to keep your story straight. This doesn't mean you'll read directly off of the deck and hope your investor doesn't fall asleep. Instead, you'll create an entire pitch designed to use the deck as a memory prompt and a way to lead the conversation.

Imagine your deck is a script for an outline. Slide one reminds you to introduce yourself. Then you describe your problem. The deck offers imagery that you can't describe verbally. Further, the deck can bring up data and other information that you might be missing in your presentation. You can simply glance at the deck and add the info that you missed.

Do not under any circumstances write out your pitch on your deck. Your pitch - the verbal part of your presentation - is augmented by the deck. The two work together to give your arguments more force and value. They can never be the same thing because, by definition, your pitch deck assists you in your presentation and is not an exact copy of your presentation.

Your deck should allow you to clearly and concisely describe your product through images, designs, and (some) text. You should be able to use the deck as a stand-in for your actual product.

People will often stare at your deck while listening to you. This will break their concentration and so you should be ready to pull it back to your voice as you pitch.

This assumes, of course, that you have created a deck that contains pertinent and important information. If you've filled your deck with a lot of data and text, you're going to end up panicking, jumping from slide to slide and from your memorized script to some kind of ad-libbed commentary. A bad deck can break your concentration while a good deck can help focus that same concentration. Further, the audience's eyes often drift back to the deck. Even if your verbal pitch is flawless, they will be busy trying to understand a fifteen-column spreadsheet you put up between two pieces of clip art.

A pitch deck lets you run someone through your idea quickly. You could even send the deck, tell them to visit page four, and then explain your point using images and text. It's a cheat code for your pitch.

Ultimately, your deck is only as good as your facility with words and your confidence. Without confidence, a deck becomes just another tool - neither good nor bad but when misused it can be disastrous.

Your Pitch Deck is a Way to Share Your Idea With the World

A deck is the new business plan. The deck is the lingua franca of modern startup investment, and people will ask for it constantly. You must be prepared to deliver it.

You wouldn't randomly send your business card to strangers in the mail and hope someone responds. But if you create a compelling deck you can convince people to respond. When you share your deck with someone, it means you expect a call-back, a second look, a chance.

That said, a good deck can stand on its own. It is a way to describe your project without resorting to a meeting and it's a way to show someone what you mean without having to fire up your beta software or even show them a working product.

How do you send your deck out into the world? The easiest way to do it is to create a link inside your own domain - something like mycoolsite.com/deck - that links to a DocSend page or simple PDF.

Do not add a "deck" link on your website, however. Decks are used in very specific situations and leaving a wide-open deck for all comers is not specifically dangerous but definitely confusing. We've seen some entrepreneurs who turn their deck into their websites. This isn't a good idea as, again, the confusion associated with seeing the 10-slide format in an odd setting could frustrate visitors. The pitch deck is not for public consumption.

You can use a deck as a teaching and media tool. Many companies will often share their decks with journalists who then use them as an example of a deck that raised a few million dollars. This kind of PR turns you and your team into thought leaders and by making your deck special you create a very unique opportunity for yourself and your team.

The deck also lets them check out your idea without investing the time to speak to you about it. If this seems problematic you're right: a deck that leaves your hands is akin to a toddler that is loose in a candy shop. The deck, like the toddler, can give everyone a bad impression and, more importantly, cost you a lot of money.

What NOT to do

Here are the five DON'Ts of pitch decks:

1. Don't use default templates. A pitch deck has to look great. If it looks like just another PowerPoint document then you're going to be seen as an amateur. Not comfortable with design? White background with stark black letters will go a long way to defining your pitch. Consider using easy-to-read san serif fonts like Helvetica.

2. Don't save the good stuff for last. An investor will look at the first three slides of your pitch deck and know, almost instantly, what they want to do with your company. Those first slides must be streamlined and contain both compelling text and visual information. Those slides include the title and startup description, the description of the problem, and your solution. Everything else is gravy.

3. Don't depend on text. No one wants to read your manifesto. Instead, they want to see screenshots, diagrams, and graphics. A chart is always better than saying "We grew around 500% in the past year." Share your growth, your revenue, and your success visually, when applicable.

Remember: in the end, your investors want to understand your product and, what's more, believe that you can sell it at a profit. Your pitch deck should contain that promise in the form of screenshots, product shots, mockups, and designs. Also remember the 80/20 rule: humans take in 20% of the information you share and the rest - the context, the design, the images on the screen - make up the other 80%. This means that you will have very little control over the process of sharing complex ideas in a 10-slide deck. Instead, you want to make that 20% of attention paid to your ideas as clear as possible.

4. Don't make your deck boring. It's a hard job, I know, but trust me: a boring, plain deck shows investors that you aren't invested in your idea. Your deck is the first step on the road to your corporate identity. Use it to define who you are as a company and what you stand for. If you're playful and irreverent, let that come through in your deck. Staid and buttoned-up? Show that in your deck. As you grow, you can use the ideas you embedded into your deck and turn them into your corporate aesthetic and colors.

5. Don't add extraneous information. Many startups add citations, massive charts, and competitor slides that overwhelm the reader. Don't do that. Instead, offer a balanced look at the company through your deck. Show, don't tell.

Unless you're asked, many decks don't require profit and loss statements or use of proceeds slides. We'll describe the method for adding these later on in the book but for now, you are simply describing the problem and selling your solution.

Your pitch deck is a chance to make a good first impression on a group of people who don't necessarily want to even communicate with you let alone give you money. Your deck is the foot in the door.

A word on NDAs

When it comes to NDAs and investors "stealing your idea" you can relax: it will never happen. When you pitch your startup you are selling yourself and your team, not an idea. Ideas are cheap. They can be replicated and discovered easily and your idea is worth nothing without your expertise and experience. Never make an investor sign an NDA. It's not professional and makes you appear paranoid and fearful.

Remember: you own your startup. You should be able to make the case that you and only you can build it to fruition. Unless you've invented a jetpack for kittens, your idea is probably indefensible and anyone - including your biggest competitors - can build it easily. What you bring to the table is what really sets you apart. Without you, the idea is meaningless. Therefore your goal is to ensure your investors that without you the idea is impossible.

There is a concept called the secret sauce: what is the secret sauce that makes your idea better than every other one? This could consist of your experience, your skills, your intensity. If your idea is so incredible that it deserves an NDA then you're probably not an entrepreneur and instead, you're working within a larger organization with the resources, money, and time to solve big problems. By all means, patent your startup idea if you must but an NDA at an early stage of your startup is literally a red flag to any investor. It says, simply that you are either an egotist or not focused on an investor's success.

Who should have your deck? The bottom line is simple: random people shouldn't have your deck. You can send it to an investor or interested party who might pass it along to others but do not put it in a place that is publicly accessible. Your mileage might vary when it comes to who sees your deck and when, but generally, you want to have full control over the experience.

Still dead-set on an NDA? Be ready for lots of pushback and be ready to pay a lawyer to fruitlessly attack those who you think might have wronged you. Simply having an NDA puts you into a different frame of mind which, in the end, will become unhealthy.

The OSPTR Model

Before we begin we will want to understand what we are doing and what we want when we pitch. This requires the Orientation/Problem/Solution/Tangible   Results worksheet. The OSPTR worksheet describes our goals in detail and allows us to build a framework around our thinking when it comes to our product and business.

Before we can build anything we need to have a baseline. This OPSTR worksheet is your outline for beginning both your one-sheet deck and your 10-slide deck. Use this chapter as a way station in the process of communicating your idea in visual form.

The OPSTR worksheet is quite simple. Draw a box and slice it down the middle. Put the labels Orientation, Problem, Solution, and Tangible Results on the left side and leave the right side for your text. You'll do another sheet just like this one but with a few more fields in a moment.

OPSTR Part 1

The top of the worksheet contains the following:

| Orientation | An abstract of our product. This is a very short description of your product. This would count as a minute-long pitch and can be used as such in conversations. Our advice? We use this simple formula to generate our one-line pitch: [Your Product] is a [what it does/what it is] that focuses on the [size of market] [target market]. We intend to use our [secret weapon] to access this [monetary size of | Frog Identifier is a tool to identify frogs using AI and machine learning that offers the five million global frog enthusiasts a better way to identify frogs. We use a specialized model designed by Stanford PhDs to tap into the $5 billion market of professional herpetologists.

Or

WriteManager offers simple document management solutions to 200 million small business owners |
| --- | --- | --- |

	market] dollar market by offering [what your product solves].	*and employees and is dependent on our patented machine learning and categorization algorithms.*
Problem	A short description of the problem you are trying to solve.	*Frog fans have no real way to identify frogs in the wild except through catch-and-release tactics.*
Solution	A short description of the solution.	*Frog Identifier uses an AI algorithm to identify frogs automatically.*
Tangible Results	What will happen when the product is launched.	*When Frog Identifier is popularly available it will change the way hobbyists find and catalog frogs. This will result in millions in revenue for the business.*

Notice something interesting: this sheet contains everything you need to prepare your pitch. It tells the world who you are, explains the problem you need to solve, and describes your secret sauce. If you only read this at a pitch-off, for example, you'd have exactly what you'd need for a basic pitch. By focusing your thoughts in this way you can quickly and easily prepare a pitch that will give your audience an exact description of who you are and what you are doing. This is your 1-minute pitch.

OPSTR Part 2

Next, let's expand our pitch using a few key points. It is an expansion of your part 1 and will allow you to build your pitch with even more detail. It is basically what you will say to investors when you sit down with them to talk about your business. In fact, this is your 3 to 5-minute pitch.

When writing this pitch use colloquial language and simple terms. The descriptions should be usable even without a slide deck in front of you. Once you're done with the pitch, you should be able to recite it from memory at any time and in any environment, including at a trade show or in an elevator.

| Introduction | This is basically your abstract, above. Tell the investor who you are and introduce the important members of the team. | *Frog Identifier is a tool to identify frogs using AI and machine learning that offers the five million global frog enthusiasts a better way to identify frogs. We use a specialized model designed by Stanford PhDs to tap into the $5 billion market of professional herpetologists.* |

What are you building?	Describe the product in detail. How does it work? What are all the moving parts? What is the secret sauce?	We use AI and machine learning to assess frog types and their various calls. Our team, led by Dr. Alfred Croaker, has created an app that lets you point your phone at a frog to identify it instantly.
The available investment opportunity	What are you raising and at what valuation? What kind of investment are you accepting?	We are raising $1 million on a $10 million dollar valuation. We are raising using SAFE notes.
Risks	What are the risks associated with this product? Who are your competitors? Who are your customers? Be honest: by showing investors that	Our closest competitor, Frog Finder, uses GPS to find frogs in the wild. Our customers are also very picky when it comes to app colors and so we must run many detailed QA tests

	you are aware of the risks you reduce their fear and uncertainty about your capabilities.	*with test subjects.* *We may have also overestimated the global interest in frogs.*
Your goal	What does the world look like when you're done with your product? What changes?	*When we are done frog identification will be as easy as Shazam's music-identifying system.*
Year 1	What does the company look like in year 1, including the current time? Do you have an MVP? Customers? Does the product work?	*We currently have an MVP in the App Store that can identify if something is or is not a frog. The next version will be able to identify green frogs only.* *We have 500 users who are paying $4.99 a month for our frog/not frog app.*
Year 2	What will happen after you	*With funding, we will finish our full*

	gain funding? What will you do with the cash? How many people are waiting for this product? Finally, what will investors get if they invest?	*app and begin selling the complete service for $19/month. We currently have 10,000 people on our mailing list who are willing to pay for the new app.* *Profit for investors should be within the 20% range yearly if all of our calculations are correct.*
Exit state	What will happen when you have completed your goal? Will you sell? Will you go public? What are your plans for the future?	*Dr. Croaker would like to expand the technology to help identify newts and slugs. In the future, the team plans to take the business public.*

Feel free to print and pass out this document to everyone in your company. Have them all answer the questions with what they feel are the most important aspects of the business. If you're just starting out then you shouldn't have much trouble collating everyone's ideas and producing a coherent deck.The resulting Rashomon of ideas will allow you to crystalize your business and prepares you for the pitch decks we will build in the next chapter.

Use this document as an outline for building your own OSPTR document in preparation for the next steps in the pitch deck process.

| Orientation | An abstract of our product. This is a very short description of your product. This would count as a minute-long pitch and can be used as such in conversations. Our advice? We use this simple formula to generate our one-line pitch:

[Your Product] is a [what it does/what it is] that focuses on the [size of market] [target market]. We intend to use our [secret weapon] to access this [monetary size of market] dollar market by offering [what your product solves]. |
|---|---|
| Problem | A short description of the problem you are trying to solve. |
| Solution | A short description of the solution. |
| Tangible Results | What will happen when the product is launched. |

Introduction	This is basically your abstract, above. Tell the investor who you are and introduce the important members of the team.
What are you building?	Describe the product in detail. How does it work? What are all the moving parts? What is the secret sauce.
The available investment opportunity	What are you raising and at what valuation? What kind of investment are you accepting?
Risks	What are the risks associated with this product? Who are your competitors? Who are your customers?
Your goal	What does the world look like when you're done with your product? What changes?
Year 1	What does the company look like in year 1, including the current time. Do you have an MVP? Customers? Does the product work?
Year 2	What will happen after you gain funding? What will you do with the cash?

Exit state	What will happen when you have completed your goal? Will you sell? Will you go public? What are your plans for the future.

The One-Pager

We will begin dirty work of building a deck with the simplest pitch, the one-pager. One-pagers are single page documents aimed at giving a high level view of you product. Some VCs prefer them to pitch decks so we will show you how to make one. In fact, many VCs will ask for a one-pager first and follow up with a deck request.

A one-pager is a compressed pitch deck and by making one you can gather your thoughts and attempt to describe them precisely in a more compact document. Further, you could feasibly take much of your one-pager and expand it into your pitch deck just as you will use your OSPTR document to build this one-pager. Creating a one-pager is a great exercise for the creation of your longer deck. The one-pager will help crystalize your thinking and reduce the complexity associated with deck building in general.

You will give one-pagers to interested investors. Never send your 10-slide deck prematurely. Instead, send the one-pager and ask them if they'd like to see more. As with every "rule" we offer in this book your results may vary but keep in mind that we have seen the pitching experience from both the investor's side and the startup's side. These rules of thumb we offer will help you and your potential investors communicate clearly and quickly without confusion.

The Parts of a One-pager

A one-pager is a one-page presentation document or memo. It usually consists of a structured document of about 500 words. It is not a narrative, memo, or story. Instead it is a prospectus - it tells your reader exactly what they need to know about a particular product.

What follows is a very simple one-pager. If you've been thinking about your startup for any length of time it you should be able to produce your own one-pager in a single sitting. It assumes very little in the way of design savvy or even writing skill and instead distills everything you need to share in a complete and compact package.

Not all founders feel comfortable writing, especially in English. We recommend having your one-pager - and your pitch deck - proofread by a native speaker before sending it anywhere. A minor grammatical mistake can mean the difference between an enthusiastic investor and a cold shoulder. The same goes for your 10-slide deck: a single typo can sink your chances.

This is a one-pager we made for a small startup that did video delivery. It was actually very successful in engaging investor interest.

▶ HypeHop

Site: hypehop.com
Email: team@hypehop.com

HypeHop is a new tool in the growing field of *attentive marketing*. We've created a system that lets marketers address viewers directly and it rewards dedicated users by paying them outright for their attention. We believe the system can be used in multiple environments and we are currently working with partners to bring HypeHop powered tools to the marketplace.

Team

John Biggs - CEO

Former East Coast Editor of TechCrunch. Involved in cryptocurrencies since 2010. Extended experience in analysis, company grading, and investigative accounting.

Joe Smith - CTO

Joe is an experienced full stack dev with 20 years experience in building complex video products.

Screenshots

WHY

HypeHop is a system that rewards viewers with a small amount of BTC for watching a video. We call this "attentive video."

The key to HypeHop's magic is the ability for the system to watch you as you watch a video. Because we need to ensure users are watching these videos to collect their cash we've created a component that watches your face and tracks your emotions as you watch the video. The system pays out in BTC and accepts BTC to post videos. This is because there is no sane way to accept micropayments in USD or any other fiat currency.

The product is truly the first of its kind. We posit that the average user is sick of giving up digital autonomy but will do so if rewarded in a real way.

WHY US

This team is expert in media, facial recognition, machine learning, and UX. Our goal is to create a company that will build and/or license this technology to partners who will use the tools we've built to work on their own attentive solutions.

TOTAL TARGET RAISE: $750K - 18 MONTH RUNWAY
- $375k in product development
- $300k in biz dev, product marketing & PR/events
- $75k in legal, accounting, insurance and administration/ops
- Round Terms - $5m Cap, 10% Discount, Convertible Notes, Minimum Check Size $25k

The Logo and Contact Information

The first part of your one-pager is your logo and contact information. Your logo should be fairly stable at this point and you should add a high-resolution copy of it to the top of your one-pager. Don't have a logo? Get one. Fiverr or Upwork have plenty of folks who can make a simple logo for a few dollars. Get a few alternatives and pick your favorite.

Next to the logo we can place your website and email address. Make sure you have a domain to go with your company. Do not add a Gmail or Yahoo address although for some security companies a service like Proton Mail could be considered the safety-conscious route. That said, if your email address is davematthewsfan99@hotmail.com then you should probably head over to the registrar ASAP.

The Team Section

The team section describes the major figures in your company. It is not a complete company directory. We recommend focusing on C-level employees including the CEO, the Chief Operating Officer, and Chief Technical Officer. Essentially you want to prove that you have the team to do the job.

Your goal in this section is to show off your skills. Even though you might not even have a product at this point your mission is to convince a cynical audience that you and your team have the skills and experience to build your product. This isn't your resume. Instead it is a bulleted list of relevant skills that will make someone sit up and take notice of your potential.

The Screenshots

These are smaller screenshots of your product aimed at showing, in an instant, how your product works. Don't have screenshots? Mock some up or have some photos taken of your prototype. This section is a "nice-to-have" but if you can't provide any screenshots at all then you should probably reconsider fundraising and pitching. Investors and interested parties need to know you have something even if it is ultimately vaporware.

The Abstract

This is a very short description of your product. This would count as a minute-long pitch and can be used as such in conversations. Our advice? We use this simple formula to generate our one-line pitch:

[Your Product] is a [what it does/what it is] that focuses on the [size of market] [target market]. We intend to use our [secret weapon] to access this [monetary size of market] dollar market by offering [what your product solves].

See the OSPTR Model chapter for more examples.

Why?

This is answers the question "Why is this product needed?" The goal of this section is to describe how the product works succinctly and clearly as well as describe some of the "secret sauce" that makes your product superior. Don't give away too much - this is a teaser for investors who might want to request your pitch deck later.

Why Us?

This explains why you and your team are the best for the job. How much experience do you have? Why did you decide to take on this project? What are your goals? In short, explain why people should trust you to win in this space.

Raise Targets

Valuations differ across the country and around the world. If you haven't yet decided on a valuation, assume something like $4 to $8 million dollars for early investors.

There are many reasons people invest in early stage startups. But in most cases, it will not be altruism. It will be because they see an opportunity to make money. Or it will be out of a fear that if they don't invest in your company or service, they will lose out on a future opportunity to make money.

This also sets your valuation – the amount you are "pricing" your company at in the beginning. For example, you can say "We are looking at a $2 million investment at an $8 million pre-money valuation" which simply means you want to sell a fourth of the company. You can then explain how you'd like to raise it. In most cases, you will say "We will raise on notes," which means you will use the SAFE note, a "loan" document popularized by 500 Startups. Raising is beyond the scope of this book - you can check out my book Get Funded! for more information on this topic.

Still confused by valuations? Ask a startup mentor to help you with the valuation. Even at an early stage, it is important to know what you are worth. In fact, I'd recommend that you and your team go through a startup accelerator. Many accelerators give you access to a clearer valuation after completion. For example, the Alchemist Accelerator in San Francisco "gives" you a valuation of

$8 million pre-money because of how prestigious it is. Accelerators that are difficult to join often tell investors that their startups are worth far more than the average startup in your area.

The "Deal Sheet" Format

There may be a case where you are asked to produce a deal sheet for an investor. This kind of request is rare but you should be ready for it if an investor asks. Therefore, we'll show you what they look like and how to prepare one.

A deal sheet is a one-pager that investors send to each other to describe your product. In most cases you will not be producing this kind of document but if you are asked it helps to know the format. Further, building a deal sheet for yourself allows you to crystalize your pitch even further by reducing all of the important aspects of your company into one or two lines.

We do not recommend sending a deal sheet instead of a one-pager. A deal sheet is a very specific tool used by investors. That said, you should be ready to fill out a deal sheet if asked.

If you must send a "deal sheet" instead of a traditional one-pager, what follows is a simple deal sheet used by investors to trade deals. These deal sheets are as simple as the one-pager but offer an assessment based on various startup categories. In all honesty you will probably be creating this kind of memo for an investor to share with other investors, and the various ratings - as shown behind each headline - are defined by the investors themselves. That said, there is nothing stopping you from formatting your one-pager in this way.

BAKER HALL CAPITAL
DEAL SHEET

Name: **FrogFinder**

URL: http://frogfinder.com

DECK:

https://docsend.com/view/hereismydeck

CEO
Name: **Jim Johnson**

Email: jim@frogfinder.com

DESCRIPTION
FrogFinder solves the "instant delivery" of frog data problem for suburban areas (not city centers), using a "mesh" of scanning systems to identify frogs.

STATUS
Solution: **Product Built, Initial Testing**

MARKET
Location: **Global**

Focus: **US**

Vertical: **Delivery**

FUNDING
Raising $4 million Seed Round with $15 million valuation and 20% discount. SAFE note.

TOP 3 NEEDS
1. Purchase of equipment, and hiring of personnel for initial US market.

2. Establishing partnerships with frog lovers and frog clubs.

3. Establishing a user base.

FOUNDER - RATED 4/5
Jim has extensive e-commerce experience in Europe and is currently employed as a Senior Developer building frog identifying tools for NASA.

MARKET - RATED 5/5
Frogs are a $1tn market in the US. The Frog ID market is currently 10% of total AI spend and is growing quickly.

TRACTION - RATED 5/5
The complex software that manages FrogFinders identification systems is complete and has been extensively tested using real-time testing data over the three years of its development

COMPETITION - RATED 4/5
There are many companies currently pursuing the quick frog ID market, but most are constrained to urban areas. Froggy.ai is the closest comparable, using an AI model designed in South America, which often misidentifies U.S. frogs.

WHY NOW - RATED 5/5
Frog ID has advanced 10 years in the space of 18 months, and customers have become much more demanding. They now want good prices, and the kind of response times they have come to expect from higher-end tools.

This deal sheet follows the one-pager design but includes a number of additional headings. The document above is a deal sheet that was sent out by a VC partner to other VCs. Therefore you'll probably have to use the VC's "letterhead" on the top. Your company name should not feature prominently on the top of the page.

Company: This heading describes the URL and adds a link to the longer deck.

CEO: This section gives the name of the CEO and their email address. There are no other employees mentioned in this section because, at its core, a startup hunting for funding is solely represented by the CEO.

Description: This is a short description of the startup similar to the mad lib described above. Make it as succinct and simple as possible.

Status: This section describes the company's current status in the market. Are you shipping product? In Beta? How many users do you have? Offer a very simple, very concise description of this information.

Market: Where are you selling? Where is your primary market? What is your primary company focus? This is often a few simple words. For example, a B2B company with a founder in the US and a team in Ukraine would write: **US-based customer focus. US and Ukraine-based developers. Primary vertical: B2B sales.**

Funding: What is your current funding? This includes angel rounds and sweat equity. Your goal here is to describe what money you have in the bank and what you are looking for from an investor.

Top 3 Needs: What do you need from an investor. What is missing in your project? Do you need customers? Help with sales? Assistance in marketing? What can an investor do to ensure that their investment becomes a 10X or 100X return?

Founder: The founder section describes the founder's skills and experience. Why is this person the best person to solve the problem associated with the startup? The goal is to convince the investor that the founder is the only person who can solve this problem.

Team: This allows founders to describe the rest of the team. Focus primarily on founders that are clearly important to the company's mission. This is not a laundry list of employees but a short list of the most skilled members of the team.

Velocity: How fast is your startup moving? What is the "FOMO" associated with your company? What can investors expect in terms of forward motion when it comes to company growth?

Market: What is the total addressable market for your solution? How many people need your product? Will you build other markets because of your product?

Traction: What is your current company status? This is similar to the Status section above but should include specific numbers including customer numbers, email list size, and anything that shows a dedication to growth.

Competition: Who is your primary competition? How far along are they? Don't include an exhaustive list, just the companies that you and your team have in your rearview mirror and that could gain on you over time.

Why Now: Finally, why is this company important? How vital is this company to the marketplace? To the founders? To the stakeholders? Use this section to describe what happens if this company doesn't work: what will change? What won't happen? This is probably the most important section because it describes your roadmap in clear, concise language.

Again, the average investor should build one of these for you if they are serious about helping you. That said, it's good to know how to make one if necessary.

The one-pager is the first step in building your full pitch deck and the thoughts and ideas that went into creating it will be very helpful when you begin building your larger deck. As we move through the OSPTR process to the one-pager to the deck, you should begin having a better understanding of how to communicate your project simply and directly.

Building Your Deck

Now let's talk about your 10-slide pitch deck. Unlike your one-pager, the 10-slide deck is far more detailed and requires much more preparation. That said, everything we've done before this chapter will help us build our pitch deck far more quickly than if we had jumped straight into the ten-page pitch.

Your pitch deck is the first thing most investors will see about your company and, sadly, it's often the last. As we said, your pitch deck is your calling card and it helps make your first impression. That's why it's a key part of every founder's utility belt. Therefore, your deck must be precise, readable, and compelling. It's a tall order, definitely, but not impossible.

First, let's talk about the difference between a pitch deck and any other deck.

Most of us have had the rare privilege of having to sit through long and agonizing PowerPoint presentations. These massive files consist of dozens of slides jam-packed with terrible clip art, confusing graphs, and long, unedited content, with a speaker simply reading the words on the screen. This type of PowerPoint presentation, as we noted before, is referred to as corporate PowerPoint," and it's difficult to break the CPP habit once you get into it. PowerPoint decks are frequently used as crutches in the workplace, as a means to prepare for a meeting without having to memorize or grasp the subject.

The CPP is defined by endless text on a white background, inscrutable diagrams and charts, impossible-to-read tables, and bold confidentiality disclaimers along the bottom of every slide. While this is great when you're pitching at the Dunder Mifflin annual meeting, it doesn't work when you're pitching an investor.

You've probably been building CPPs for your entire career. It's time to stop. I've seen decks in a corporate setting that were 77 slides long. They were literal tomes of endless prose and weird animated GIFs. If you're building those for your startup, stop.

CPPs work when you're in a big organization and the stakes are far lower than in the startup world. A pitch deck is essentially a tool you're going to use to raise money for your big idea. Treating it like a CPP is silly at best and dangerous at worst.

Corporate decks are information rich and often designed to be read, not skimmed. Take a look at these slides:

US Wireless Market – Q2 2010 Update

Executive Summary

The US wireless data market grew 6% Q/Q and 22% Y/Y to exceed $13.2B in mobile data service revenues in Q2 2010 - on track so far to meet our initial estimate of $54B for the year.

Having narrowly edged NTT DoCoMo last quarter for the first time, Verizon Wireless continued to maintain its number one ranking for the 1H 2010 in terms of the operator with the most mobile data revenues (though the difference was thinner than the amoeba membrane). The total wireless connections for Verizon were almost 100M with 92.1M being the traditional subscriber base. Rest of the 3 top US operators also maintained leading positions amongst the top 10 global mobile data operators.

Sprint had the first positive netadd quarter in 3 years and has been slowly and steadily turning the ship around. T-Mobile did better on the postpaid netadds but overall additions declined again. The larger question for the market is if 4 large players can stay competitive. Generally, the answer is no. But these are different times and there are a number of permutations and combinations that are possible.

The US subscription penetration crossed 95% at the end of Q2 2010. If we take out the demographics of 5 yrs and younger, the mobile penetration is now past 100%. While the traditional net-adds have been slowing, the "connected device" segment is picking up so much that both AT&T and Verizon added more connected devices than postpaid subs in Q2 2010. Given the slow postpaid growth, operators are fiercely competing in prepaid, enterprise, connected devices, and M2M segments.

Data traffic continued to increase across all networks. By 1H 2010, the average US consumer was consuming approximately 230 MB/mo up 50% in 6 months. US has become ground zero for mobile broadband consumption and data traffic management evolution. While it lags Japan and Korea in 3G penetration by a distance, due to higher penetration of smartphones and datacards, the consumption is much higher than its Asian counterparts. Given that it is also becoming the largest deployment base for HSPA+ and LTE, most of the cutting edge research in areas of data management and experimentation with policy, regulations, strategy, and business models is taking place in the networks of the US operators and keenly watched by players across the global ecosystem.

As we had forecasted, the tiered pricing structure for mobile broadband touched the US shores with AT&T becoming the major operator to change its pricing plan based on consumer consumption. We will see the pricing evolve over the next few quarters as the US mobile ecosystem adjusts to the new realities and strategies for mobile data consumption.

Modeling customer dynamics

- ☐ **Model 1: Lost-for-good (Dwyer 1989)**
  - – Two-state model: customer / no customer
  - – Customer who has left never returns
  - – Modeling issue: lifetime analysis

- ☐ **Model 2: Always-a-share**
  - – multi-state model
  - – More complete dynamics (includes Lost-for-good dynamics)
  - – Modeling issues: describe state changes
  - – Classical model: Markov Chains (Pfeiffer/Carraway (2000), Piersma/Jonker (2000), Tirenni (2005))
  - – Basic assumption: the probability of a state change („hazard rate") does not depend on the past, in particular not on the sojourn time!

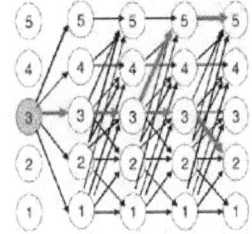

 **Swiss Institute** OF SERVICE SCIENCE

Everything here, from the font to the text density to the incomprehensible images to the copyright notice at the bottom, is indicative of a corporate deck. The goal of a corporate deck is to impart as much information as possible to a group of people who already understand the problems associated with a business or even that particular meeting. If you whip out one of these decks at a 3pm meeting at your massive corporate headquarters, chances are everyone in the room can understand exactly what you're talking about in the context of a long-running corporate relationship. Further, given that it's 3pm, most of the stakeholders involved will probably be too sleepy after lunch to pay much attention. That's exactly what you don't want when it comes to a pitch deck. Think about it: if you try to use a corporate deck on a person who is not a stakeholder and is, in fact, adversarial to your cause then you're sunk.

Building your 10-slide deck

The easiest way to start a non-CPP deck is to use one of Keynote or PowerPoint's prefab templates and then have it redesigned by a professional designer. This is your starting point but definitely not your ending point. This simple, stark presentation will allow for maximum creativity.

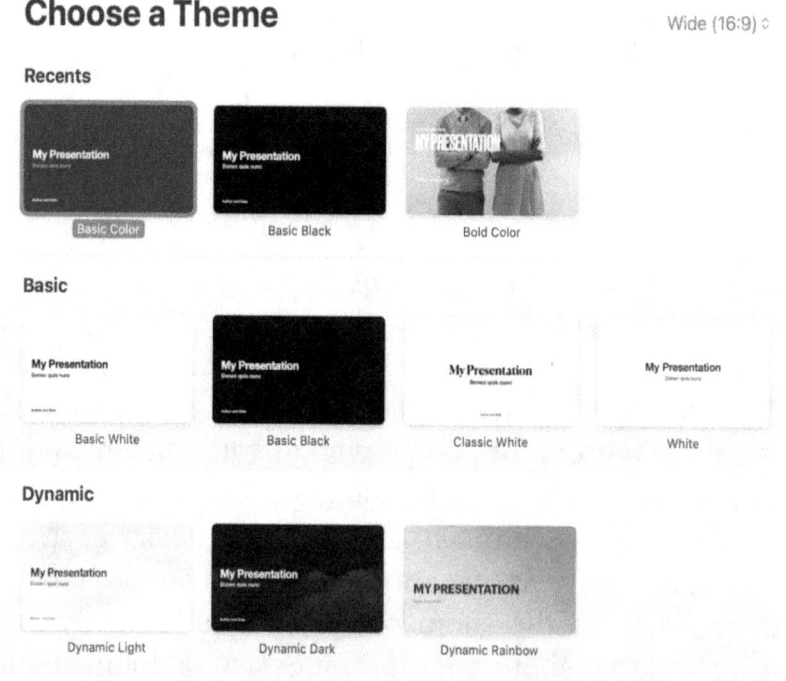

Pick a presentation from the Basic offerings, not the Dynamic Rainbow.

The non-CPP deck rule of thumb is to ensure a maximum of forty words per slide and as few extraneous tidbits as possible. These tidbits can include NDA reminders, privileged information disclaimers, parenthetical sourcing. No one needs to know you got the fact that 80% of dogs like to eat bacon from the Pets.com 2020 Sourcebook for Veterinarians. That said, all of this data should be available at your fingertips as necessary.

There is a school of thought that suggests that you have to show your sources. If you're uncomfortable, say, stating a statistic without citing your source in small text at the bottom of the slide then by all means do so. That said, you'd do well to avoid the impulse to put much else on a slide then is absolutely necessary.

The Goal of a 10-slide Pitch Deck

To get funding for a business or idea, you will need to **show there is a need for that business or idea**, and then **prove *you* are the one to do it**. This is your primary mission and anything that strays from that mission is ancillary to the goal.

Most corporate decks are aimed at getting people to **move** in one direction. A pitch deck is aimed at getting people to **think** in a new direction. A CPP is a map. A pitch deck is a manifesto.

Pitching isn't all about spreadsheets and financials. It's about getting others to become emotionally connected to your idea. Your pitch deck is your personal story - it describes a world that will be better because your product or idea exists. If you can't get someone to invest, you can use your pitch deck to at least get them to tell others about you and perhaps connect you to other potential investors.

A pitch deck is also a script for a performance. You will use it to bring your potential investor or supporter through the same process you went through when you created your startup. If this sounds like theater, that's because it is. And it's your job to pitch a story with real villains, likable heroes, and a happy ending that makes people want to see more.

A pitch deck is also not just for when you are seeing investors. It's also useful for finding clients and partners. If you can explain your business in a few words and then close with your "ask," namely what you're raising and at what velocity, you are likely to get an answer that results in a good outcome.

A pitch deck is also a great way to focus the mind on your business. Creating a deck ensures that before you pitch that you've got your story straight. Your deck will inform your email pitches, your pitch style, and how you answer investor questions. It is a very powerful tool for any entrepreneur.

Before You Start

There are a number of popular theories and best practices on how to build the perfect presentation, but these are usually focused on business meetings with colleagues or potential customers and partners. These presentations require more slides, more graphs, and more information. As we discussed before, those types of presentations are exactly the opposite of what we are trying to produce. When meeting with investors, you must reduce and streamline. When you are asking someone for money, the biggest mistake you can make is to throw a giant haystack at them. Your job is to hand-deliver the needle.

If an investor chat is like a date, then the deck is your Tinder profile. It sets the stage for what is to come and becomes a road map for the interaction. It tells the investor what to expect but doesn't define you. The investor will "swipe right" on your deck if they see something they like.

A few years ago, marketing guru and venture capitalist Guy Kawasaki wrote about his 10/20/30 Rule of PowerPoint, which states that a presentation should contain no more than 10 slides, last no more than 20 minutes, and contain font no smaller than 30 point. Although he wrote this rule back in 2005, his advice about being short and concise should be something you take to heart whenever building a presentation.

Ultimately, a presentation is less a script and more a guide to how you will structure the conversation. This of course assumes the meeting flows in a linear fashion. More than likely, it won't. You should expect questions, interjections, and possibly not having enough time to get through all your slides. This is why it's imperative that you front-load your presentation with the most important information.

Some rules before we begin:

Use images. Arresting images turn a pitch deck from a boring grind into a fascinating journey. Use services like Unsplash.com to find cool images that are applicable to your business. Almost all of the images you will see here are from Unsplash or from elsewhere on the Internet. Don't be afraid to hunt around.

Always proofread your deck. This is becoming easier with grammar and spell checkers but remember: one misspelling or one poorly phrased sentence is an instant "No." Your deck, in reality, is your first product. Make it amazing.

Get a native speaker to check your work. If you are an international startup, you have to have your deck proofread by a native speaker of English. We've seen far too many decks get torpedoed because of one typo or grammar mistake. In a perfect world, no one should be judged on their English prowess but the startup world communicates primarily in English and any mistakes are easily and instantly noticed by savvy investors. Potentially you won't have this issue but it's not worth the risk.

Getting Started

Now that we've discussed why we need a 10-page deck, let's build on.

A winning pitch deck proves three key factors in every meeting.

Market Opportunity	Your Solution	Their Opportunity
Make them believe in the opportunity.	Make them believe you (and your team) can win.	Make them believe *they* can win by investing in you.

As we build our deck, remember those three points. Too many founders forget, for example, to explain the opportunity available to the investor. Remember: investors are giving you money in order to make more money. Any presentation that doesn't address this is useless.

Let's get started.

Open a blank PowerPoint or Keynote document. Use a very simple style. Don't worry about design at this stage. Just create the slides and add the titles below. These are just placeholders to remind you of the purpose of each slide.

1. Title Page

2. The Problem

3. The Solution

4. The Product

5. The Revenue Model

6. The Challenges

7. The Team

8. The Financials (and The Ask)

9. The Opportunity

10. The Road Map

11. Appendix (Optional)

Create the Content

Using our fictitious technology company FrogFinder as an example, we will demonstrate how to fill in the content for each slide in your presentation.

Slide 1: Title Page

The simplest slide you will ever create. Add your company name and logo, your CEO's name, and some contact information. (We like to add a cool photo on the first page if we're doing a public pitch, but investor pitches can be far less flashy.) That's it. Only nine slides to go!

SLIDE 1 – TITLE PAGE

Slide 2: The Problem

Often referred to as "setting the stage," this is arguably the single most important section of your presentation. Whether you are looking for people to crowdfund your food truck or a VC to invest in your healthcare app, if you fail to make them believe in the problem, then you will never get them to invest in the opportunity.

Using both facts and relevant anecdotes, you must answer these two key questions: What are the key pain points and what is the market opportunity?

- Pain Points: Your goal here is to get the investor to quickly agree to a simple, factual narrative. For example: Using our FrogFinder example, we will address how hard it is to identify frogs with any degree of accuracy. This is very simple to understand.

- Market Opportunity: You got them to agree to the problem, but do these issues impact enough people or businesses to create a real opportunity (to make money)? Use facts and figures that quickly illustrate the size of the market you are going after. This is where you begin to create FOMA ("Fear Of Missing Out").

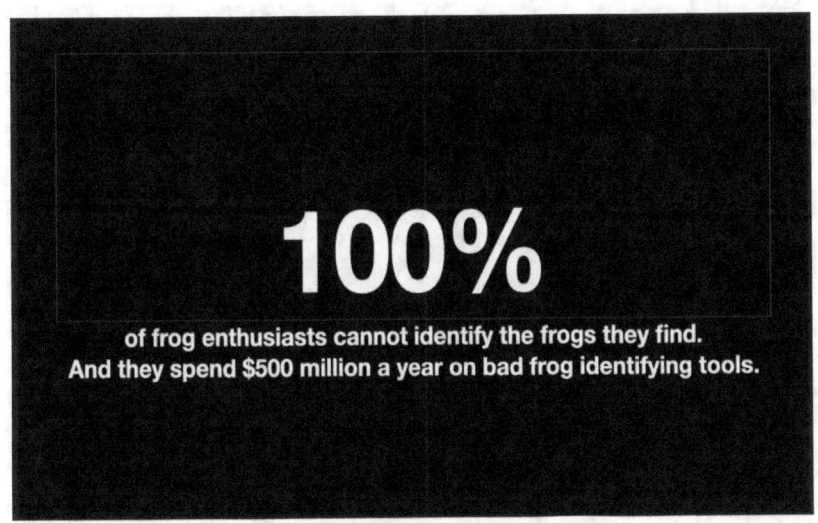

100%

of frog enthusiasts cannot identify the frogs they find.
And they spend $500 million a year on bad frog identifying tools.

Note: If you have a meeting with an investor, you should assume they have done some basic due diligence about your space. Use your time wisely, and make sure every fact you place on this slide is there ONLY to set up your specific solution.

Slide 3: Your Solution

Using simple language, state your company mission and then briefly describe how you will accomplish it. Keep in mind that you are not writing a script here. You will have different talking points for each slide.

As you can see, we have a simple tag-line - "AI Solves the Frog Crisis" - and then we offer a few interesting data points. Further, we've added a fun image to this slide. Start thinking about design in the early stages in order to inspire yourself or your designer when it's time for a proper edit.

Keep this slide simple and use it primarily as an introduction to the next slide: The Demo.

Slide 4: The Demo

Our MVP app works!

- Identify any frog in seconds
- Receive important frog information
- Freemium model is already generating $4,000 in month of revenue
- Future updates will create Frog-Identity-as-a-Service

This section of the presentation will depend on your company or product offering. If you have a taco truck, you might have photographs of the truck, copies of your menu, or photos of the food itself. If you have a new invention, you should consider sharing 3D renderings or unveiling a physical sample or prototype during the meeting. The key here isn't to overwhelm them, but to leave them wanting (and asking for) more. You also still have six more slides to go and you don't want to use up all of your time.

Since we haven't yet finalized the FrogFinder mobile app, we will share some mockups of how the interface will look. We aren't showing everything – just screenshots that bring to life the most powerful aspects of the app. In this case, we have one screenshot and a few bullet points about the app itself. You're going to want to add more screenshots if you have them.

Slide 5: The Revenue Model

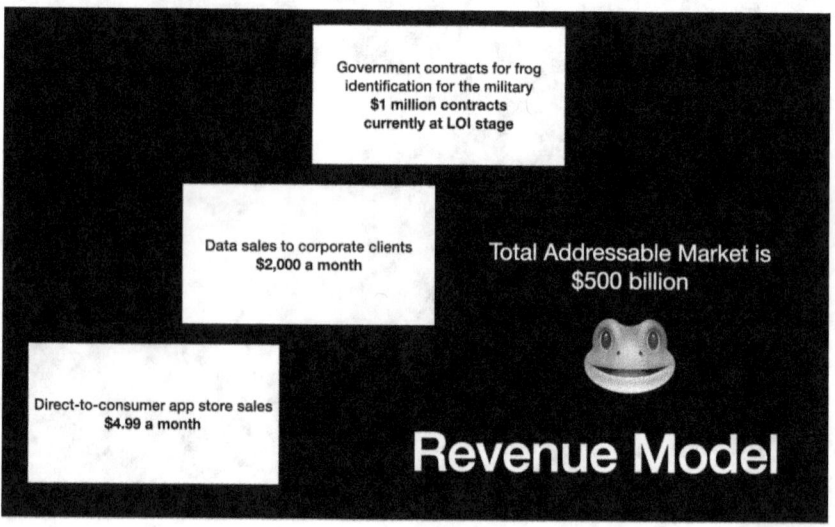

This slide answers two simple questions: How will you make money? And how much money have you made thus far? This slide should explain how you make money better than your competitors do and what your "secret sauce" is in terms of building the business. If yours is a more traditional business, a simple outline of your current and expected revenues should be sufficient.

Some founders like to add information regarding their current investment and valuation but don't be too hasty in sharing these numbers. Many investors will want to set their own terms for early rounds. Create a deck that you can easily modify or create a version with your current valuation and without.

In our example slide, we showed potential sales for multiple channels, including massive contracts with the U.S. government. Obviously, a frog-finding app might not rake in that much dough but it's nice to dream!

Slide 6: Competitors and Challenges

Let's be honest. If it's obvious enough to you that this opportunity exists, then it's perhaps obvious to others. So why isn't this opportunity being addressed? Why are others failing?

Going back to your OPSTR analysis, it's time to be "strategically transparent." We say strategically because this isn't a therapy session at which you will reveal all of your issues. The goal here is to show your potential funder that you have a real grasp of the internal and external challenges to your business, and how you plan to deal with them.

Competitors and Challenges

- Frog Finder competitors include:
  - FROGMASTER
  - FrogIDer
  - FrogApp
- All these apps use human generated identification systems that are slow and don't work
- We are the only app that uses AI
- Currently looking for a marketer to enter the lucrative Asian frog IDing market

Many founders create a "bullseye" slide here to rank various competitors on a number of axes. Your startup, obviously, always lives up and to the right when compared to other startups. The bullseye slide is arguably a bit tired these days but feel free to use it if it helps argue that your product is superior to competitors.

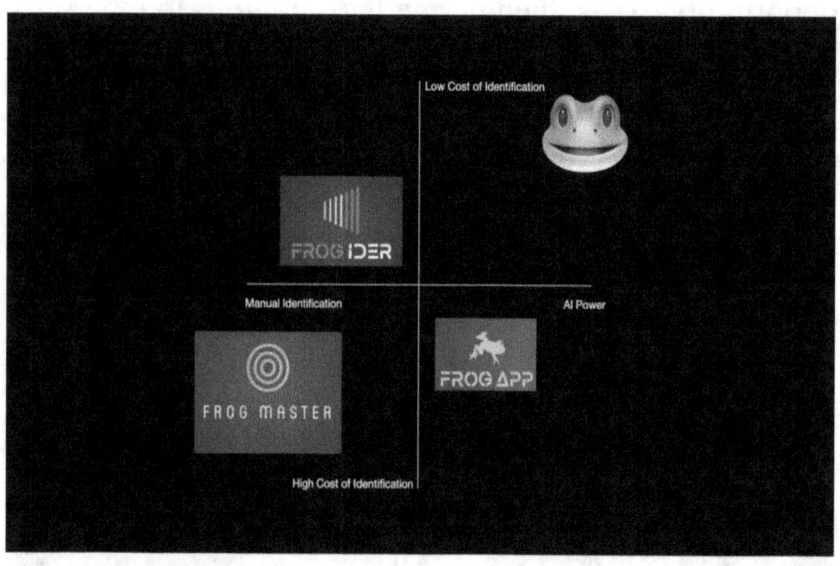

Slide 7: Your Team

Creating a team slide might not seem particularly challenging, but this will be one of the most critical parts of the presentation. Investors *invest* in two things: people and opportunities. This slide should make the investor feel confident that if they give you money, it will be well managed.

The goal of any successful team introduction slide is to showcase a successful combination of education, real-world experience, and good ole entrepreneurial spirit. If you didn't graduate from an Ivy League school or previously helm another successful startup, you will need to double down on showing your and your team's entrepreneurial spirit.

Investors are looking for three distinct people on your team: a hustler, a hacker, and a hipster. This means the hustler will be out getting customers and investors, the hacker will be coding or building, and the hipster will be designing the whole thing. If you're missing one of those roles, you might need to rethink your launch. That said, many founders can take on two or more of those roles at once... but not for long. Be ready to hire someone or find a co-founder as soon as possible.

Using the chart below we have outlined some of the most common scenarios and suggested strategies for presenting you and your team. See which scenario best describes your team.

The One-Person Team	This is the most challenging scenario for any entrepreneur. Let's assume the investor loves your idea, they will now be looking for relevant experience and a successful track record in your previous roles. They will also be looking closely at your personality and whether you're passionate enough to keep things moving forward in the bleakest of

	times and pragmatic and ethical enough to make the tough calls.
Best Friends Team	Many great business ideas have been hatched over a beer or long dinner with friends or a significant other. But investors don't want to deal with a many-headed Hydra or have an entire investment be put at risk because of a breakup. In this scenario, you will need to show that one person is ultimately in command of the day-to-day aspects of running the company. You may also need to prove that there are legal contingencies in place that protect the business in the event of personal fallouts.
Missing Link Team	If you are missing some key players on your team, don't try and hide this. You can either wait until

	you have the right people in place to take a meeting or let them know that some of the funding will actually go to filling these critical positions.
Corporate Elite Team	Working at a startup is much different than being employed as an executive or middle manager at an established company. They are messy and scrappy and require a smaller team working longer hours with fewer resources and a strong probability of failure. In short, it's not for everyone. If your team's experiences come only from established companies, you need to make sure you are highlighting key initiatives and successes that bring their scrappy, entrepreneurial spirit to light.

What to put on a team slide? Keep in mind that you are going to speak to this slide, so keep it simple and stick to the basics.

- Name
- Title
- Current/past relevant experience
- Education

Focus only on those key team members who will prove to investors that you have the talent in place to not only run your business, but also to deal with the critical challenges you previously laid out in your presentation. Add photos; they have a humanizing effect.

Slide 8: The Financials

Feature your projected two-year financial model. This slide is a classic case of damned if you do, damned if you don't. If you don't put this slide in your pitch deck, they will ask for it. If do put it in the deck, chances are they won't believe the numbers. So, include it, but keep it simple.

The following, for example, is a standard revenue model for a new startup that aims to gather cash via app sales. As you can see, nearly everything is accounted for including salaries, dev costs, marketing, and hosting. In our decks we like to add founder salaries at about month six, thereby ensuring the investors know that they won't be paying you out of pocket for your work. In this case we show $2,000 a month salaries for the three C-level execs which is a bit saner for those bootstrapping their projects. Be ready to defend your decisions here, especially your revenue projections.

Revenue Projections
Year 1

Y1	Month 1	Month 2	Month 3	Month 4	Month 5	Month 6	Month 7	Month 8	Month 9	Month 10	Month 11	Month 12	Totals
Revenue	$5000	$8000	$8000	$12000	$15000	$18000	$21000	$24000	$27000	$30000	$33000	$36000	$237000
Salaries	$6000	$6000	$6000	$6000	$6000	$6000	$6000	$6000	$6000	$6000	$6000	$6000	$72000
Dev Costs	$10000	$10000	$2000	$2000	$2000	$2000	$2000	$2000	$2000	$2000	$2000	$2000	$40000
Marketing	$10000	$10000	$10000	$10000	$10000	$10000	$10000	$10000	$10000	$10000	$10000	$10000	$120000
Hosting	$2000	$2000	$2000	$2000	$2000	$2000	$2000	$2000	$2000	$2000	$2000	$2000	$24000
Total													-$19000

Year 2

Y2	Month 1	Month 2	Month 3	Month 4	Month 5	Month 6	Month 7	Month 8	Month 9	Month 10	Month 11	Month 12	Totals
Revenue	$36000	$36000	$40000	$44000	$48000	$56000	$60000	$90000	$100000	$190000	$200000	$250000	$1150000
Salaries	$6000	$6000	$6000	$6000	$6000	$6000	$6000	$6000	$6000	$6000	$6000	$6000	$72000
Dev Costs	$10000	$10000	$2000	$2000	$2000	$2000	$2000	$2000	$2000	$2000	$2000	$2000	$40000
Marketing	$10000	$10000	$10000	$10000	$10000	$10000	$10000	$10000	$10000	$10000	$10000	$10000	$120000
Hosting	$2000	$2000	$2000	$2000	$2000	$2000	$2000	$2000	$2000	$2000	$2000	$2000	$24000
Total													$894000

If this seems like a lot of data, you can easily simplify this and adding a more detailed spreadsheet to the appendix. If you're worried you don't have this data, don't be. Simply make your best guesses based on your experience in the industry. We've created a sample version for you to download and use on the website.

Slide 9: The Opportunity

Many refer to this slide as The Ask. This is where you explain how much you are raising and how much you are asking for.

As we discussed earlier, there are many reasons people invest in early stage startups. But in most cases, it will not be altruism. It will be because they see an opportunity to make money. Or it will be out of a fear that if they don't invest in your company or service, they will lose out on a future opportunity to make money.

This also sets your valuation – the amount you are "pricing" your company at in the beginning. For example, you can say "We are looking at a $2 million investment at a $8 million pre-money valuation" which simply means you want to sell a fourth of the company. You can then explain how you'd like to raise it. In most cases you will say "We will raise on notes," which means you will use the SAFE note we describe in *Get Funded!*

Ask a startup mentor to help you with the ask. If you leave an investor meeting without an ask then you are most likely going to get good advice and no check. At least have an ask ready to go when you are sitting at the conference table.

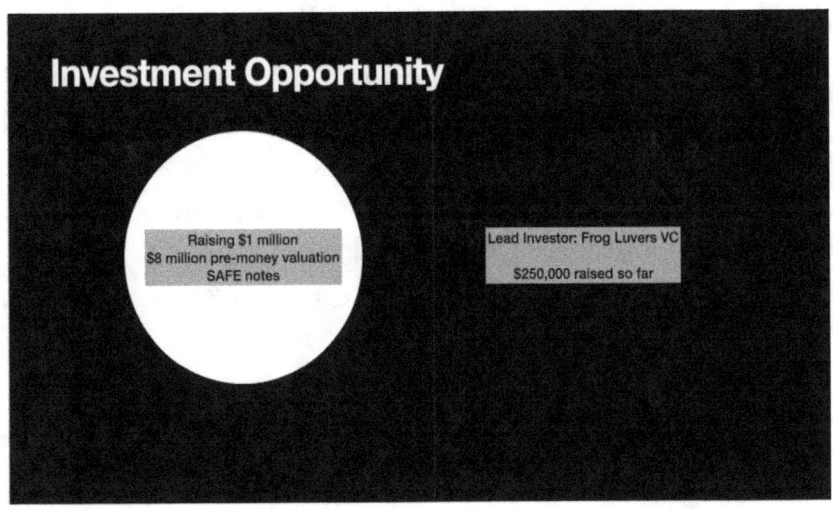

SLIDE 11 - OPPORTUNITY

Slide 10: The Road map

At this point in the presentation, you need to discuss where you are in the process of launching (or expanding) your product or service. Here are a couple of ways to show that.

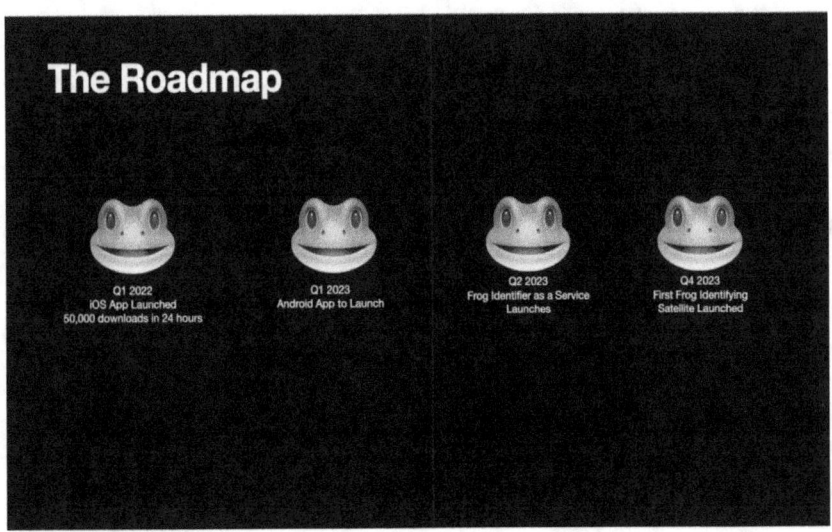

Be Brief, But Carry a Big Appendix

The key to a good presentation is to be concise and brief, but you may find yourself failing by not being prepared for the follow-up questions. This is why it's a good idea to be ready with extra slides in your appendix. We can't tell you specifically what would be relevant for your particular idea or pitch, but based on our own experiences, here are some thought starters:

- More detailed financials
- List of current customers (B2B)
- Media quotes and press review highlights
- Quotes from key customers
- Examples of marketing collateral
- Photography, video – anything that brings your idea to life
- Detailed competitive audits
- Detailed bios of each team member

Sample Deck Breakdown

What follows is a simple 10-slide deck. It was built for a company that raised a small amount but closed due to the difficulty of building a two-sided market. That said, it was a great idea. I've cut it into pieces here and will explain each slide in detail. Note the consistent design from slide to slide and the use of humans in the photos. Decks must be visually interesting, even arresting. If you're not a designer, hire one to build something similar. If you're comfortable with design, be sure to pass your deck around to friends who can give tips on design, layout, and language.

We recommend creating two decks – one that includes your succinct 10-slide "focused" presentation" and another longer "appendix" deck that includes financial targets, budgets, and the like. As we noted in the last chapter, the appendix deck is what you send to investors who want more data. This may also include fawning descriptions of your entire team and whatever else you think an investor with more time and patience would be interested to read. This longer deck has an appendix and is designed only for investors who require more information after seeing your first deck.

Slide 1 - **The Introduction** - This slide focuses on the "vibe" your company uses to define itself. In this case we have a single tourist looking over a city scene and we open on a human figure, something to ground the experience in reality for the reader. Further, we offer a single line of text that tells us exactly what the company does.

Think of this slide as the poster for your startup movie. It should be bold and clear and tell part of your story in a way that will make readers want to know more.

Remember when we said pitching was story-telling? Well this slide is your exciting book cover beckoning your reader from the airport shelf.

THINK ABOUT IT:
- THERE IS NO SINGLE, SANE WAY TO BOOK A TOUR ONLINE
- PAID TOUR GROUPS ARE TOO BIG
- THE EASIEST WAY TO FIND A TOUR? A PIECE OF PAPER IN THE HOTEL LOBBY.

Slide 2 - The Problem - What is the problem you are trying to solve? What is the customer pain point you are attacking? This is a description of the world before your product and it should resonate with the investor in a real way.

OUR GROUP TOURS
- SMALL GROUPS (8 PEOPLE MAXIMUM)
- GUIDES ARE PAID MUCH MORE THAN AVERAGE
- TOP GUIDES LOVE OKOLI BECAUSE THEY CAN FOCUS ON THE TOUR, NOT THE LOGISTICS.

Slide 3 - Your Solution - This slide describes your

product. Here's where you become Superman or Superwoman, swooping in to save the day. In this slide you offer a bold and clear look at what exactly your company does.

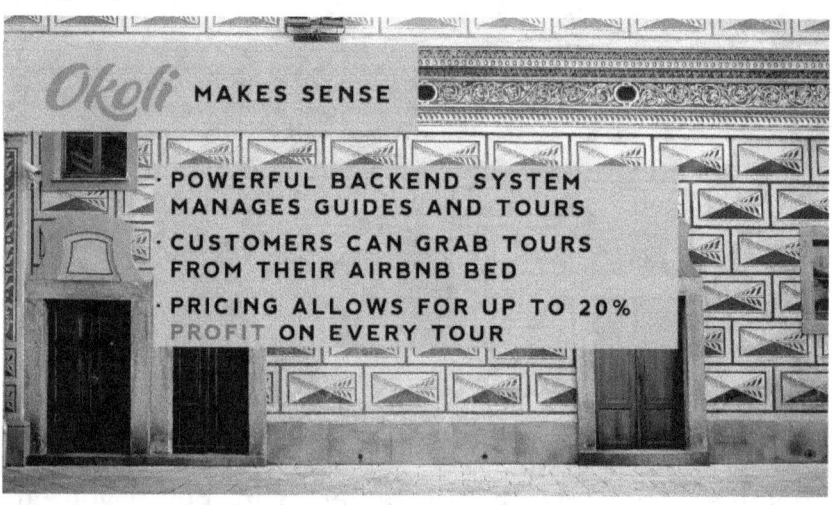

Slide 4 - Why We're The Best - This slide describes why your product is better than anything else in the market.

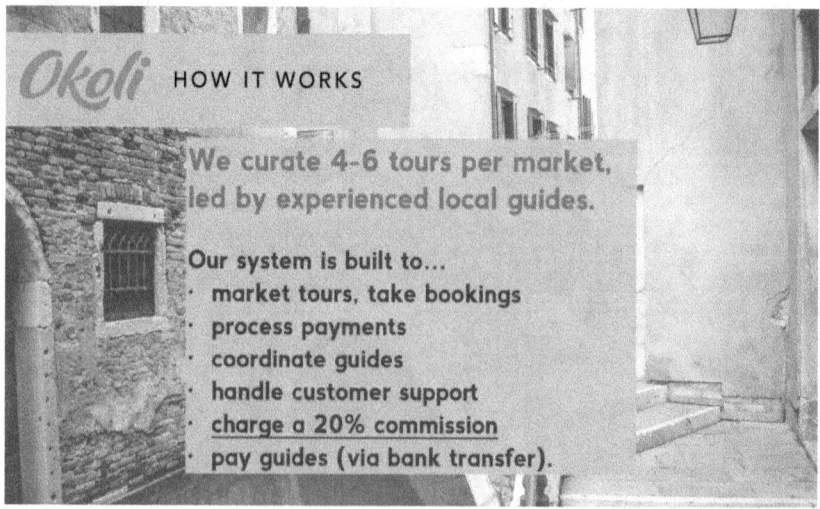

Slide 5 - How it Works - This describes how the product works in more detail.

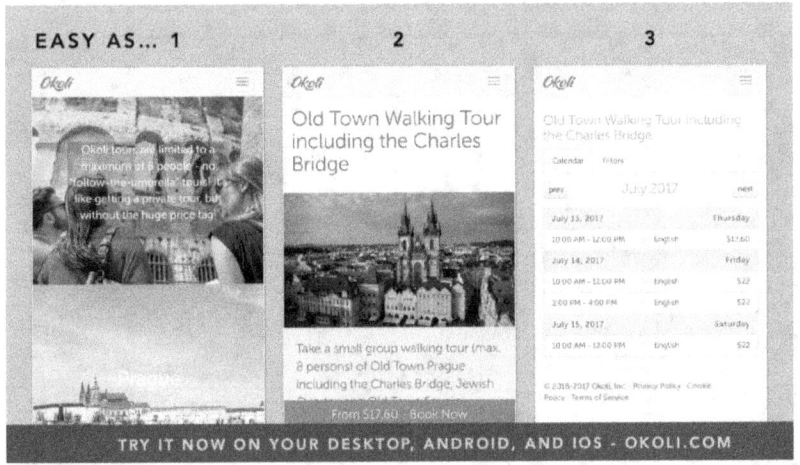

Slide 6 - The Demo - These are screenshots directly from the app or product. These will allow anyone with this deck to either imagine or even try the app in real time. Notice that in this case the app is available for download immediately, a call to action that allows investors to try before they buy.

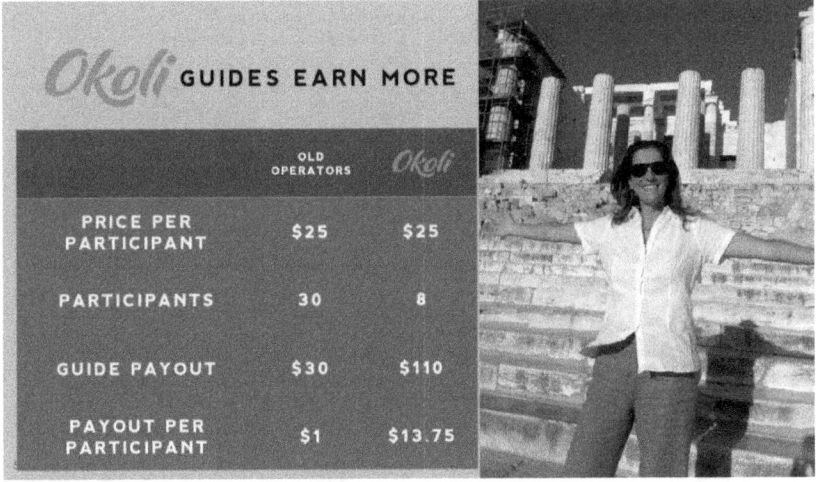

Slide 7 - Financial Model - Here's how you make money. The goal is to describe how your product makes more money for you and your users.

Slide 8 - The Competition

Slide 9 - The Team –

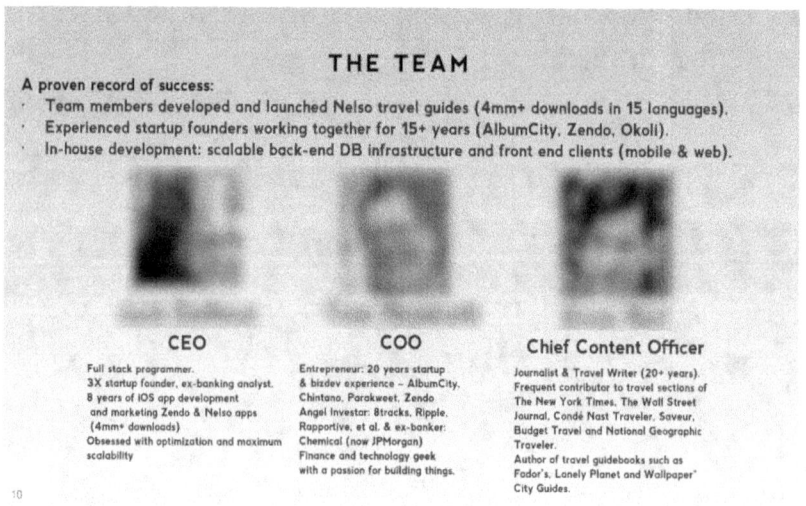

Slide 10 - The Contact Sheet -

Again, we encourage you to have your investor deck professionally designed. What does this mean? It means a designer should create a visually pleasing template using specific fonts and images. Decks with lots of pictures stand out in a sea of grey text, and decks that are arrestingly readable are far superior to decks that look like you used the default formatting found in PowerPoint or Keynote.

Once you're done with your deck, look for designers online at Fiverr and other art services. Expect to pay a few hundred dollars; more if it's a longer, appendix-laden document. Don't go crazy, though. Chances are your global design will evolve over time, even your business name and logo may change.

How to Build Confidence

You're in the room. People are listening to you. You are wearing your best hipster hoodie or a suit and tie. All you know is that you're ready to tell your story.

Here's how to survive.

First, remember to breathe. Pitching is one of the most nerve-wracking experiences you will ever have. We humans are used to being judged silently. Facing down a panel of experts who have the power to make or break your company is something completely alien to us. That said, remember: nothing in that room can go wrong for you. Even if you don't raise a dime and even if your pitch flops with one group of people, rest assured that you will have made an impression on everyone in the room. Your mission? To make it the best impression possible.

Remember: most people don't even get as far as you have. You've got a deck, you've got a product, and you're moving forward. That, alone, is worth kudos.

So you're in the room. **You brought your computer as well as an HDMI adapter and HDMI cable.** These two items may be less important over the next few years - wireless presenting is humming along fine - but it's better to be safe than sorry. Want an even bigger dose of preparation? Bring an Ethernet cable and adapter. The "demo gods" often like to ruin opportunities and so you should be ready for every contingency.

You set up your gear. Your computer is connected to the overhead monitor. You are seated facing the audience. You are calm and smiling.

Does all of this sound a bit too meditative? Trust us -

pitching is very hard and by using every tool at your disposal you're assured a good experience.

1. The Small talk

Don't jump directly into your pitch but begin with two minutes of small talk. Discuss the room, the drive up, recent (non-partisan) news. Make note of things you see on the walls, even in a virtual call, and ask your audience about their interest in those things.

Is there a guitar on the wall? Comment on it. Is there a specific and unique piece of art? Ask about it.

Perhaps you're not the best at small talk. Assign a team member to be in charge of that task. Add commentary when applicable and eventually say something like "Well, let's take a look at the deck…"

2. Describe what will happen

Before you begin you will lay out your mission, your goals, and the expected outcome. You will also talk about how much time you have: "We have 30 minutes, I see. I think we will have plenty of time for questions."

In terms of explaining your mission, you're going to have to make a choice. In many cases beginning with the amount you are raising or even a valuation during the beginning of the pitch might put your audience off, especially if you don't match their specific needs in terms of check size or company stage. If you are certain that you can openly discuss this before the pitch deck because the investor and your needs are aligned, feel free to open with the ask.

Try this script:

So thank you, [investors]. I appreciate your time. We have half an hour so I propose the following:

I'm going to pitch for five minutes. I'll give you the basic deck and we can dig further as needed. Then I'd like to spend fifteen minutes on questions and answers. Then we should spend the last ten minutes so we can ask you questions about your firm. Finally, we'll define the next steps. Sound good?

Although this kind of pitch sounds canned, remember: the people you are talking to have seen an inordinate number of pitches and you might be number six that day. By laying out the roadmap and by reminding investors what's coming next you control the conversation. Further, it lets the investors relax because they are being led forward by a capable and intelligent leader - you!

3. Pitch

Run through your pitch as described before. Don't embellish, don't add or subtract. Just run the pitch. This process should be the same for almost every pitch but have someone else on your team listen and watch the investors to see if they are dozing off or particularly excited. This will allow you precisely improve your pitch once you're done.

Your pitch is an opportunity for your investors to think. While you're talking they will be imagining different opportunities and, worse, imagining potential problems with your project. They will have preconceived notions of your idea and they will think about products similar to yours that they had seen before. All of this happens instantly and instinctively.

Allow investors to ask questions and process their own thoughts during a pitch, even if it breaks your concentration. The key is to answer their questions directly and concisely, without offering explanations that weren't asked for. It is important to practice only answering exactly what is asked, and to be prepared to answer "I don't know" to questions that are problematic. This can open up an opportunity to demonstrate what it's like to work with the founder.

4. Make the ask

Ask for money. State, unequivocally, that you are raising cash and why you need it now. Do not forget that this is a business meeting. You are there to tell them that you're looking to build something real and that you need their help (and cash).

5. Close with your questions

When you talk to investors it's helpful to have these questions ready after your pitch.

Who makes the decision to invest?

What is the average amount you invest in a startup? What is the maximum? How small a check do you write?

Is there anyone else you know that I should meet?

Would you be interested in meeting our team?

Where do you prefer us to be located?

What is your preferred investment vehicle?

What is your investment timeframe?

These questions will help you refine your follow-up answers and will help focus your investors. Frame the conversation succinctly at this point but explain what you just pitched and what you want. This helps to ensure that everyone is on the same page and that the conversation is productive. Thank your investors for their answers and for asking questions to clarify the next steps. Be sure to thank everyone in the room! A kind word can make or break a pitch.

5. Follow Up

Follow up on a pitch meeting on the same day. Why not send follow-up materials including your appendix, use of proceeds, and a copy of your deck. Also include access codes to your product, if applicable. If the investors are ready to write a check, a pre-signed SAFE note should be included with a deadline. Use an e-signature program to automate the process and send daily reminder emails if they agreed to invest and haven't followed up. If there is no activity after a few days, it is time to reach out to the investor via some other method. Don't give up!

The one-pager Cheat

If you are an experienced founder with a built-in network of investors, your one-pager might be the only thing you need to build your first round. The one-pager is what is called a narrative memo and describes exactly what you're building with few frills, bells, or whistles. It is a simple document that any investor can understand.

Here's how to use the one-pager as a fast and easy way to run your pitch efforts.

1. Create a one-pager and write a three-paragraph memo outlining the data in that one-pager. This document is a text memo similar to the kind that Jeff Bezos asks his managers to supply instead of depending on presentations. The memo is for your eyes only but, again, the process of writing out a memo describing each section of your one-pager allows you to put into words all of the various things spinning around in your founder brain. In our world, writing out a presentation is the first step before pitching simply because it is the simplest and most sure way of ensuring you are telling the right story in the right way.

Your story should consist of the following pieces of information:

- Describe the new situation in the world that is forcing your company to exist on a macroeconomic level. What has happened globally that is forcing you to act?
- Describe the new situation in the world that is forcing your company to act on a microeconomic level. What is your company doing to be important?

- What is the implied need for these new consumers? What are you going to offer them in order to react to these implied needs?

Create your abstract, as described above:

[Your Product] is a [what it does/what it is] that focuses on the [size of market] [target market]. We intend to use our [secret weapon] to access this [monetary size of market] dollar market by offering [what your product solves].

Include a description of three paying and happy customers who will offer testimonials about your product and, as mentioned above, include a team description to prove that your crew is exactly the crew to get the job done.

The key to these memos is clarity and simplicity. You must structure a story around your business that shows it has depth, value, and potential. Think about the "movie pitch line" for your business: *Ghost* meets *My Dinner With Andre*. In this case, you're going to offer something simple that makes it abundantly clear to the investor what you are doing. Think "Fitbit for dogs" or "Hubspot for farmers." Three or four words max.

Investors love memos because pitch decks are elusive. A pitch deck, when done correctly, can clarify a point and do the work of the pitch. That said, most pitch decks hide your thinking behind waves of graphics and buzzwords. This book is an attempt to help you clarify that thinking and create a method for thinking about your startup in absolutely clear terms.

Need help building your memo? Use the OSPTR document you created in ther previous chapter and turn it into a series of bullet points. This can be expanded into longer text paragraphs and finally becomes your investment memo.

2. Build a list of investors. The easiest way to find investors in your area is to read a site like TechCrunch. TechCrunch often describes who invested in what startup and by hunting down competitors you can find firms that are specifically interested in your company. Remember: investors often won't invest in two of the same kinds of companies - they won't invest in two robotic car companies, for example - but if you are in the B2B space look for the investor who focuses on B2B. By digging a bit into investor websites you should be able to find a few investors who might be in your wheelhouse. You can also do searches on sites like PRNewswire where you can find funding notices by various companies, including startups. Look for words like "led by" and "funded by" in these press releases to find potential investors.

Make a spreadsheet of investors and create a plan for outreach. We recommend something like this:

First Name	Last Name	Email		Phone	First Contact	Second Contact	Third Contact	Result	Followup Tasks
Milo	Mora	mora6156@gmx.comaol.com	Dingo Partners	539-555-0276	1/2/22	1/9/22		$10,000 raised	Send Wiring Instructions
Agatha	Goudriaan	goudriaan3172@eml.cc	Brace Partner	349-555-85	1/2/22	1/9/22	1/2 2/2 2	No response	Rest art in Feb

				s	19				
Sh avo n	Mira nda	miranda4306@s peedymail.org	VCs Are Us	91 0- 55 5- 98 72	1/2 /22	1/9 /22	1/2 2/2 2	$25, 000 raise d	Send Wirin g Instr uctio ns
Ra mo n	Amp tman	ramon_amptma n7427@yepmail. net	Dor f VC	87 6- 55 5- 02 62	1/2 /22	1/9 /22	1/2 2/2 2	NEE DS LEA D INVE STO R	Call in two mont hs
Art	Men dela ar	art_mendelaar33 01@jetemail.net	Jerr y Can Ven ture s	93 5- 55 5- 78 02	1/2 /22	1/9 /22	1/2 2/2 2	No resp onse	Rest art in Feb

You'll notice that you'll want to note each outreach by date and reach out at least three times during any fundraising period. Make notes as to who has pledged cash and who might need more information or time. Also, plan for follow-up tasks including contacting the VC a month later to see if they might have been too busy to respond earlier. If any of this raises any kind of anxiety then you should be prepared for plenty of that feeling in the future. Running a funding effort is difficult, frightening, and exhausting and it is a full-time job. Be prepared for the worst and you won't be disappointed.

First-time founders might have a very hard time getting investor attention. Don't get frustrated. Once you create a working product and offer some kind of return on investment, you will quickly notice that investors will be lining up to take a portion of your company. That said, it's amazingly frustrating at first and you should be ready for this as you go about the fundraising process.

Don't give up.

3. Send your one-pager and memo. This is the trickiest part of this process. Send your memo and one-pager and ask for the investor's opinion. What do they think of the idea? What are they thinking in terms of the future of this particular industry? Remember the immortal words of Pitbull: Ask for money, get advice. Ask for advice and get money.

Not getting a response? Call the investor - if you have their number. This process is far too important to stand on ceremony. Fundraising is uncomfortable and frustrating. It consists of long periods of boredom interspersed with short periods of massive stress. It is not fun and it can damage you physically and mentally. Take it slow and follow the steps in order to ensure you're ready to pitch calmly and carefully when the need arises.

4. Know when to give up. Some ideas can't be funded. This means they are too early, too late, or the value proposition isn't clear. This doesn't mean you should quit your startup or throw in the towel. It means you need to keep building without outside investment, a prospect that sounds scary but it is actually freeing. When you're less concerned about raising capital you will focus more on building your business.

Again, don't give up prematurely but be ready to accept the inevitable if it comes down to it.

TIPS	It's possible you already have customers, so dig into what you've learned and how you plan to scale this. If you haven't launched your business or product yet, then you need to be prepared to address what you will be doing to find customers. One warning: investors do not want to see their money being used to market an idea. Get a loan if all you need is money to market. They want to invest in ideas, build products, and in some cases, provide strategic support. The best ideas, in the beginning, are low-cost or no-cost and easy to scale. For one startup I (John) created I reached out to Chambers of Commerce in various cities, allowing us to speak to many companies at once. Yelp had salespeople call countless businesses around the world in order to sell profiles. Both these

	methods were time-consuming, but they didn't require large marketing budgets. Note: It's also important to be prepared to address a secondary set of questions here: What will be the cost to acquire each new customer (CAC). A company's CAC is the total sales and marketing cost required to earn a new customer over a specific time period. If you aren't a marketing person, or don't have a marketing person on board, we strongly recommend spending some time building a plan and then addressing it briefly and honestly. You can then have more detail in your pitch deck's appendix for those investors who want to dig into this in more detail.
Q	What are your biggest challenges?

TIPS	Talk about a loaded question! Investors obviously want to vet your business for any risks that might impact their investments. But they also want to see how you and your team thinks. If you don't have an answer to something you feel is a legitimate concern, it's OK to say something like: "This is honestly not something we have spent a lot of time thinking about. I'd love to take some time after this meeting, get with the team, and be able to provide you with a more thoughtful response. Would that be OK?" In the case of FrogDinder, they might ask about regulatory issues, legal and liability concerns, and of course technology risks.
Q	Tell me about your competition.

| TIPS | The best advice here – even if you've truly invented something never before seen on planet Earth – is to never answer this question with NONE. There is almost always a competitor or two in any space. It could be the imperfect solution your potential customer is already using. It could be a large, well-funded corporation that might just like your idea enough to enter the market. In our GoToDoc example, it's perfectly logical that an insurance company could add this feature to make additional revenue with its customers. Look at Uber, when it launched in 2009, it was a one of a kind play. But today, Uber is competing with several ride share companies such as Lyft, Via, and Juno. Pro tip: The goal isn't to win by showing you have no competition. The goal is to show you are smart |

	enough to see the obvious and not-too-obvious competitors in your space.
Q	Tell me about your team.
TIPS	There are a million great ideas, but only a few people will have the skill of turning an idea into a successful, cash-positive business. This is why investors may put more weight behind your team than your idea. We assume you will cover the basics of your team in the pitch deck to prove that you have the right background and experience to successfully run the business, but you should expect to be challenged here. Think about how you will answer questions like: What are some of the things that motivate the founders? Who will ultimately be in charge (investors won't want to deal with more than one

	person)? What key holes do you have in your present team makeup? What are some of the things your team is good at and not good at? What are your hiring plans over the next 12 months?
Q	How will you use the money you raise?
TIPS	There are generally three things outside investment will be used to cover: 1) hires to help build your products; 2) hires to help acquire customers; and 3) general costs to run the company. The answer to this question should be, quite simply: build technology, hire key team members, buy supplies, or purchase or rent real estate. Never say you will use investor cash for marketing. Barring the lone wildmen or women who don't care where their cash is going as long as

	you are moving forward, admitting that you will use their cash for marketing is very dangerous. Why? Because marketing is a sunk cost. Spending their investment on marketing is akin to throwing it away, at least in their eyes. They want you to use their money to build something valuable that they can sell and possibly recoup their investment on. You can't sell marketing at auction. If marketing dollars are the only thing you need, then you may want to consider other funding methods.
Q	What is your company's pre-money valuation? And why?
TIPS	Although this question tends to make entrepreneurs uncomfortable, it's going to be asked. But keep in mind, this question is really being asked to make

sure this investment is a good fit for an investor or their firm. Most investors are going to have a target for the number of early-stage companies needing seed funding vs. later-stage deals. So, in the end, as great as your idea may be, it may just not be the right time to invest. This question is aimed at seeing if your team and key shareholders (both in place and soon to be in place) will have enough financial upside to stay around long enough to make this business a success. If you are reading this book — and outside of some friends and family investment — this is probably your first investment pitch. We suggest you follow the directions in the Valuation chapter and keep this answer simple, transparent, and honest. And be prepared for a

	deeper discussion.
Q	What will you do in five years?
TIPS	As we've noted, almost every question an investor will ask will be focused on revealing how they will make money with your idea and if you are the right person to do it. So, when they ask you this question, and they will, they aren't just asking for business reasons, they are asking to get a better understanding of your personality. Do you have a long-term vision for the business? Are your goals realistic? Do you really understand the risks (to their money)? This is an excellent way to deliver your proof points again. It's OK to say you are in the business for the long term, and it's OK to say that in five years you would like to sell your business. In the end, you

	will need to be successful to execute either of these strategies, so remind them of your key milestones, any revenue you've made, and your plans to get to one of those two places in five years.

Avoiding the Know-It-All Trap

Entrepreneurs are often blindsided by investors who know - or think they know - more about the industry than you do. That said, investors – VCs and Angels – have a more generalized view of many markets and see things that heads-down entrepreneurs often miss. In fact, many investors might know great deal about your industry because they have either failed or succeeded in that same industry or they have previously invested in the same kind of company before.

Obviously, not all investors know exactly what is happening in a particular industry all the time. You, the entrepreneur, might know the industry as it currently exists, which means the entrepreneur's information could be a few years out of date. That said, experience is valuable, and be prepared to counter questions regarding the general industry. This means you need to know the facts and figures associated with your industry for at least the last five years. Think of this as the homework you need to do to pass the most basic test - avoiding the investor's BS sensors.

For example, if an investor has run a consumer-facing business, their first question will be, "How will you get customers?" Why? Because they have tried (and most likely failed) to get customers themselves. They know how hard it will be. If they failed, they will be particularly adamant about the point. If they succeeded, they will ask pointed questions to confirm that your ideas fit into their view of success.

Or perhaps you're creating a two-sided market. These are the most difficult to create because you have to bring in both sellers and buyers. The answer, in most cases, should be a simple "We already have both buyers and sellers. We're raising to ramp up to have more."

This answer - a simple "We already have customers, we need your help to get more" - is the most powerful one you can offer. It shuts know-it-all investors right up because you more likely than not did a better job than they ever did in your industry.

Do Your Diligence

Learn as much about every investor before you meet them. Do your due diligence. This is much easier in the age of social media. A little pre-meeting sleuthing will help you better prepare for questions they might ask.

Maybe you can find companies that they have already invested in. Ask the CEO for candid feedback. Perhaps you can talk to current employees of the company to understand the effects the investor had on the company, good or bad.

You should also do your diligence on the investor to make them feel at ease. Understand their investing strategies. Be ready to mention previous investments. It also helps to be aware of whether or not they have already invested in your space, something that many investors avoid in principle but will do if they really like a company. Your pitch is as much about you as it is about them.

Lastly, remember that investors are human beings and are going to have good days and bad days. If you catch them on a bad day and their questions seem pointed or even aggressive, keep your cool, stay focused on your presentation, and answer their questions as best you can.

Don't Be A Jerk

In every single book on pitching they always tell you that you need an "Ask." No matter who you're talking to, Always Be Closing, right? But when should you maybe not be closing? And when will trying to close kill your chances?

In the entrepreneurial lifecycle, there are few noticeable peaks and valleys. The first peak comes when you get an idea and begin to try to build it. This initial excitement wears off quickly when you realize the limitations of your skill and network which leads to a set of doldrums so profound that the entrepreneurial mind goes a little manic.

In this stage, which I'll call the Networking Stage, the entrepreneur wants to tell everyone about their product in hopes that anyone — or everyone — will help them bring it to fruition.

This is the first time they act like a jerk but, to a degree, they should be allowed. This early stage is very hard and you need to be stubborn, at least for the first few months.

If you're still frustrated a year into this process, then you probably need to pick a new product.

Why? Because rarely does anyone want to help and if they do, few will be able to help with the intensity you require. In fact, this is the first deep trough in the journey and one that often stymies early projects. So from day one, the entrepreneur is already angry. This is bad.

Then it gets worse. At this point, the entrepreneur may also be trying to pitch their idea to investors with little product market fit, little uptake, and only a simple MVP. Again, 99% of entrepreneurs at this point have no actual product, income, or users. They are trying to pitch nonetheless.

This is where the second stage of doldrums takes hold and entrepreneurs do something like emailing investors out of the blue to say they are missing the investment of a lifetime. Further, many entrepreneurs who are exhausted by pitching will revert to a grumpy state during the pitch. As an entrepreneur, you will hear the word "No" fifty different ways before you raise your first dollar. This is an exhausting proposition and causes many entrepreneurs to lash out.

I've been in this place many times. I've asked for cash, been rebuffed, and then attacked the investor with an intense pitch that turns off investors faster than a Facebook clone. The real problem is, quite simply, when we hit a certain level of frustration we feel that FOMO is our only ally and, 99% of the time, there is no MO to FO.

You can approach most investors only when you are in a position of power. If you have 100,000 users or $100,000 a month in revenue or a product that has just taken

TechCrunch by storm then, by all means, reach out to all the investors you can. In fact, they'll probably reach out to you. That's the trick to FOMO: you can't incite that fear in another person, they have to find it themselves.

Here's the bad part: by the time you're instilling FOMO into some Sand Hill Road type, you probably don't need their help.

So what do you do while you're in the twin valleys of despair? Well, first off don't pitch like a jerk. It ruins the investor's day and makes them write you off as a try-hard. The only way out is to build and the only way to build is to do it yourself and, when the time comes and investors are knocking down your door, you can give them a simple "No." That, for an entrepreneur, is the best feeling in the world.

Practicing Your Pitch

Your deck is done. You're ready to pitch. You and your co-founders are excited. You're planning on splitting up pitching duties, giving part of the pitch to the CTO to talk about the tech and some to the CMO about competition. You, the CEO, will manage the rest.

This is wrong.

Let's talk about who should pitch.

You, as founder or CEO are expected to pitch your product to investors and other interested parties. You are the only person who should pitch. The rest of the team should be in the room and ready to answer questions but in almost every case you are the sole person pitching.

What happens if you're not comfortable pitching or if you realize you're not great at public speaking? You can then tap someone else. You might discover that someone else in the organization can tell your story better. Pitching is an experiment. Your goal, then, is to manage all the variables in the experiment, including the person the delivers the information.

One founder I spoke to gave some interesting advice: if you end up not raising based on your pitch, give the job of pitching to someone else. This doesn't mean you should Beastie Boys it and Pass the Mic from founder to founder during the pitch as we said, that's never a good idea. Instead, maybe you allow the CTO to pitch a few times and then bring in the COO or even one of the employees. Maybe your view of the industry is too granular to be interesting or maybe your intensity is off-putting. The founder I spoke to asked his tech lead to pitch simply

Slide	Slide Goal	Example Key Messages
Title Page	Introduce yourself AND set the stage for the entire deck. You want potential investors to immediately see this presentation is relevant to them.	The frog identifying market is worth $11 billion dollars. That's billion with a "B." Everyone needs to identify frogs, from school children to Fortune 500 CEOs. And we've made it faster, easier, and cheaper for anyone to identify frogs instantly.
The Problem	You have two goals on this slide: 1) convince investors that there is a real	The current crop of frog-identifying apps doesn't work. They depend on humans to do the

	problem that needs to be solved, and 2) therefore, a real business (or money-making) opportunity for them to invest in.	hard work of identifying a frog in the wild and they cost hundreds of dollars a month. We believe there is a better way and we got our team of PhDs together to solve this problem in a real and definitive way.
The Solution	This is where you put all the previous exercises to good use. You need now say out loud what you are building and how it will solve all the issues you've outlined in the previous slide. Keep slide and talking points simple – and use the demo to get	FrogFinder is an app. It lives on your phone and connects to our 1,000,000-record AI model that has been trained on frogs from around the world including Brazil, Canada, and North America - three frog hotspots where thousands of people a day need to identify

	more granular.	frogs. Trust me.
The Demo	This is probably the most important part of the entire presentation. You have addressed the problem, now bring your idea to life. If you have a product demo, then your notes here can also be the steps you will take. If you are opening a new restaurant, bring samples of food or your menu.	I want to tell you a story about our first and best customer. Joe is a scientist in Nova Scotia and he's been using books, note cards, and a 35mm camera to create a database of frogs he's found while walking to school. The database, such as it is, costs him millions of dollars a year to maintain and he can't figure out another solution for his problem. When we showed him the first version of the frog finger app, our beta, he

was almost despondent. Can you imagine? He spent years on his project and we solved it in less than a month. Frog finding is his life's mission. He built a solution that "works" but not a solution that "just works," to paraphrase Steve Jobs.

This app will change people's lives. It's a vital app for the frog-loving community and beyond. Joe is just one of the millions of people around the world who need this app. They already

		pay millions for this functionality and offering them something for $5.99 a month is a game changer. This is the absolute first time an app like this has been available to the public and it fixes so many things in Joe's life - and your own.
The Business Model	You have explained your idea and given them an incredible demo. Now it's time to show them how it will make money.	We will make money through app sales and consulting. When we release our next product, Frog Identification as a Service, we will charge corporations a million dollars a

		year for our frog-identifying services. Finally, we will offer the first global frog identification satellite, to be launched in 2023, which will allow us to identify frog populations globally. We will charge world governments ten thousand dollars a month to access this data.
The Challenges	Using the key points you previously outlined in your SWOT analysis (Chapter 12), lay out your key challenges and be prepared to briefly discuss how you will	In the frog finding industry, there are two big issues: training AI models and finding the frogs. The good news, we have a seasoned team to manage these problems,

deal with them. This can also be used as a great transition to the next slide, as your team may have the skills to manage these issues.

including a number of PhDs in herpetology and AI model generation. We also have space engineers that are building our first satellite prototypes as well as a literal rocket scientist to build our launch vehicle.

There is also the legal aspect of false positives. We also don't want to get saddled with countless lawsuits due to false IDs, so in addition to maintaining our own insurance, we are looking for creative ways to pass liability on to

		our partner service providers. The other key challenge will be getting frog lovers to see the long-term value in our service. We want them to see us as a useful partner, not a competitor, or worse, too complicated to partner with. The good news is we have a number of smaller partners interested in using our service to differentiate themselves with their corporate customers and almost every frog lover we spoke to loves the idea and wants us to

		succeed. That's very rare in this space.
The Team	This slide may seem simple, but it's critical. Use this time to convince them you have the experience to lead this business and that you have the key team in place to take advantage of all the opportunities and deal with all the key challenges.	We have covered a lot in the last few slides, but we all know that our success here will require that we have the right team in place to take advantage of this major opportunity and perhaps even more importantly, deal with all the unique legal and compliance challenges the frog industry brings. John Biggs is an experienced founder and understands the realities of a bootstrap development

cycle. We all have run our own businesses and we have held executive positions at major firms. I've personally spent the last 20 years working with startups, Fortune 500 companies, and everything in between. We have a true 360° skill set in marketing, from PR and branding to social media and grassroots campaigns. We also have the technical chops to build everything we need to carry this organization into the future and beyond. And we've hired core team to focus on the

		most critical issues and opportunities. We have a number of open positions, but in our current stage, we want to keep things lean and fast.
The Financials	Show how much you have raised, sold, and burned. Detail your monthly or projected monthly expenditures and profits.	We've already raised $250,000. That's been enough to build our first app and we won $10,000 at a startup event in our hometown. We are looking to raise another $1 million at an $8 million valuation to complete our offering.
The Road Map	Investors like to think about the future. Tell them	This is a giant industry with giant problems.

	what you'll do in the next four quarters, especially if you raise the money.	We're ready to take it on. Our team is solid, our product works, and we need your help to take us to the next level. We expect to see profit in two quarters and similar companies in this space have been profitable in year one.
Pause	Wait for questions.	post-presentation

Prepping to Present

We could write a whole book on pitching and public speaking. Some say it's an art, but we say it's a skill that requires lots and lots of practice. There are people — Steve Jobs comes to mind — who may seem were naturally gifted at being on stage and presenting, but let's be clear: there is nothing natural about being on stage.

Jobs himself was obsessive about preparing his presentations, running through each one over and over, finding emotional notes in what amounted to a simple product demonstration. He did it because he knew that a good presentation could sell a million iPhones and each of his presentations did just that.

If you are serious about improving your public speaking skills (which you should be if you plan to pitch!), we recommend reading the book The Art of Public Speaking, by Stephen Lucas.

We would also suggest watching others. TED Talks are a great resource for some truly inspirational presentations (www.ted.com/talk).

In this chapter, we would like to focus on a set of techniques and best practices aimed at making your investor pitch more successful and ultimately less stressful and awkward for you (and the investor).

You Have to Look Good

Looks aren't everything, but they are important. We aren't talking about physical beauty, poise, or sartorial splendor. We're talking about design.

One founder we spoke to was looking for a job. At that

time, we were living in Warsaw, Poland, and she was sending her resume to a number of agencies. But she was sending her old resume, a European-style CV that looked like a cross between a report card and stereo instructions. Being a budding designer, I created an "American-style" resume with classy graphical elements and strong, bold use of fonts.

In retrospect, I will say that it looked awful, but she was called in again and again for a simple reason: they loved the uniqueness of her resume. It stood out in a pile of grey pages. It piqued the HR person's interest.

Everything you do as an entrepreneur has to have that same effect. Over the years we've seen thousands of pitch decks, and we can immediately spot the decks from people who came from the corporate world. Their decks are text heavy and poorly designed with clip art that looks like it came out of the early 2000s.

If you are serious about your business, spend a few hundred dollars on good design. We've created multiple startups that began on a plain black-and-white page and quickly morphed into beautiful, well-designed websites. The key is to think about design early before all of the founders have invested all their efforts into technology and HR.

In our demo pitch, we used the most basic of designs for clarity. You need something far more buttoned up when you finally pitch your startup. Be prepared to spend some time on how your deck looks.

Be Confident

A great entrepreneur isn't always a great salesperson, but every great salesperson can become a great entrepreneur.

The key? Confidence.

Confidence isn't swagger or bravado. It's not a firm handshake and a piercing stare. Confidence comes from knowing exactly what you want and why you need it.

The kind of confidence that successful investors look for is a fire in the belly that comes from absolute certainty. I've met founders who have walked into meetings only to be shot down immediately by investors because they didn't have the right facts, figures, and concepts at their disposal. One founder we spoke to recommended creating a list of anything anyone has ever asked you. If you are asked something you don't know, make a note of it, get the answer, and follow up with the investor. Then keep that information in your back pocket for your next pitch.

This is part of being confident: being able to recite the pertinent statistics about your industry in a moment.

Confidence also comes from skill. If you are able to code all night and can explain complex ideas simply, investors will trust you. You must have the communication skills necessary to explain your topic precisely and quickly. If you're having trouble with investors, it is often the inability to communicate your idea that is the culprit. Consider bringing on someone to help you pitch, like a dedicated CMO or a public speaking coach.

It's not merely deep knowledge that wows investors. It's the ability to explain this knowledge to them. This is called "technical communication" and it is a skill all founders must work on.

Confidence comes from lived experience. Most investors can sniff out an unprepared founder. As the old adage goes: show, don't tell. In this case, talking about a passion for nanotechnology wasn't enough. What was important was the ability to show results.

Confidence comes from knowing what you want. Everything else is just preparation for the goal. In some cases what sparks an investor's imagination is as simple as a button that calls a black car. In other cases, it's as complex as a machine learning algorithm that you trained yourself over many years. It might be the culmination of countless pop-up dinners that you held at your home until you felt ready to prepare a restaurant menu. Whatever it is, by the time you present your plan to investors, you need to be intimately familiar with all aspects of your vision. An investor can see that confidence in your demeanor, your behavior, and your communication. Cultivate it.

When Should You Pitch?

When should you pitch? The short answer is "All the time." In truth, you should read the room and assess when it is a good time to approach an investor. One journalist friend recalls being pitched while he was at a urinal. This is a no-no.

Otherwise, you should always be pitching, and you should begin pitching when you've completed your MVP.

What does this mean? You need to pitch a finished product or, if you cannot build a product until you have investment, you need to pitch a very convincing mockup and plan.

The biggest issue most entrepreneurs face is the chicken and egg problem. They need money to build a product but they can't get the money until they build a product. This is something you will have to face down and accept.

No investor will invest in an idea unless you convince them it is their idea. For example, we've met investors with an entrepreneurial bent who have been thinking about an idea for years and would put money into a business because they're been working on the same idea for years. If you can save an investor time and effort with your product, you may have a chance. Otherwise, most investors want to see a clear path to profitability.

When should you meet with investors? As often as you can. There are many benefits to meeting with investors. Money may be the primary goal of a meeting, but investors can also help connect you to other investors, potential sales leads, talent, and more. They can also provide you with advice that might help you focus your business strategy and your next pitch.

There is an entire industry dedicated to helping executives pitch and we're here to say most of them are charlatans selling snake oil. Further, there are companies dedicated to making introductions for a fee. We tell our friends and fellow entrepreneurs to never pay these fakers. Please never pay anyone to pitch for you or to act as a matchmaker. While some of these organizations are legitimate, most of them aren't. We once paid $500 to meet five Indian investors over Skype. The result? Five investors who were annoyed to talk to us and who passed almost immediately.

In other words, never pay for funding. While there are a number of methods for fundraising that involve paying an amount of money upfront including equity crowdfunding, we don't recommend them for first-time founders. The precision and focus needed to build a pitch deck and pitch it to investors is a lesson in itself.

Not everyone needs to pitch in person, but it helps to understand when and why to pitch. We've spoken to hundreds of entrepreneurs who have pitched hundreds of people, from VCs to customers to family members. They follow the Always Be Pitching (ABP) model, a technique that ensures you will always be ready to pitch at a moment's notice.

Refining Your Presentation

Sadly, most people spend more time creating a presentation than they do actually practicing. Don't make this mistake. You will need to practice, practice, and practice some more.

Step 1: Read, Refine, Time.

When you are done building your presentation, put your slides in presentation mode on your computer or tablet and read through your notes out loud, switching slides as you go. Once you've done this a few times, you may find yourself changing things, which is fine. It's normal to find that certain words written aren't going to work when spoken. Once you feel you have it where it needs to be, time it.

The average person speaks about 80 words a minute. Some speak more slowly, some more quickly, but at this point, just run through it a couple of times to see if you can get to under 20 minutes while speaking at your normal pace. If it's way too short, you may want to add some additional talking points. If it's too long, then cut back.

Step 2: Memorize and Time Again.

Keep delivering your presentation over and over until you can do it without reading your notes. Make any changes as needed. When you feel you have your final talking points memorized, time the entire presentation again to see if you are still coming in at around 20 minutes or whatever timing feels most comfortable. There are cases in which you will need to create a three-minute presentation for a startup event. Use the same technique: write out your presentation, memorize it, and time it. As you become more comfortable with your script, you may start speaking faster. You may need to try slowing down a bit at this point. While speaking, try looking at different objects in the room – a picture, a chair, your dog! This will come in handy later when we discuss the importance of eye contact.

Step 3: Record Yourself.

Whenever possible, put yourself in the audience's shoes. A great way to do this is by simply hearing and seeing yourself giving the presentation. It's easy to just focus on the sound of your voice; don't worry about that. In this exercise you should be 1) listening, really listening, to the content of your presentation and 2) looking for behaviors that are distracting (unnecessary hand movements, awkward posture, ums and ahhs, etc.) Make the necessary corrections and deliver (and record) the presentation again. Repeat this process until you are satisfied with what you see.

Step 4: Practice with Distractions.

During a presentation, there may be many distractions. People coming in and out of the room, phones going off, and even people who may seem less than engaged. All of this can throw off the best public speakers. For this exercise, turn on both the radio and TV and do your presentation. Have friends or family bother you during your presentation, asking aimless questions or asking for clarifications. Create difficult situations when you practice, and you'll be ready for them in real life.

Practicing Your Final Presentation

Tip: Practice in front of others.

Speaking in front of a mirror or an empty room will never prepare you for presenting to an investor. So, gather 2-3 friends and family members in a room around a table, and deliver your presentation. Do one sitting and one standing up. Most of us feel most comfortable presenting while standing -- the range of motion is freeing. However, you will often be presenting in closed rooms where you can't get the advantage of standing. You want to practice in both situations.

Getting honest reactions and feedback from people you trust will allow you to bulletproof your presentation. It's also good to be aware of things you may have done (both good and bad) when speaking in front of others that you didn't do when delivering the presentation alone. Make sure to time and record yourself presenting. When nervous you may speak faster. If you or others notice this, do it again and slow down. You will also want to use these videos later in this chapter to spot any other issues.

Tip: Leave it alone for a while.

Take a few days and forget about your presentation. Then practice some more. With new eyes, you may find yourself changing a few words here and there, and that is OK. Just make sure you are staying within the 20-minute mark. Practice your presentation at least twice a week to keep it fresh in your mind.

Preparing for the Investor Q&A

Investors aren't going to base their decision to invest in your business on a great presentation. They are going to make decisions on how well-prepared you are and how fast you think on your feet. They will do this by asking you questions. You should absolutely expect to be interrupted during your presentation and getting questions about issues you might have planned to speak about later. Under no circumstances should you avoid answering (or at least acknowledging) tough questions or telling an investor that you will get to their question later in the presentation. They are asking questions because they are engaged, and you are there to win them over. If you are in the introduction part of your presentation and they would like to know about the team, go to the team slide. When done, go back to where you were and keep going.

To prepare, use the Q&A you've created and practice using the similar process you did for the presentation preparation above.

Step 1: Read and Refine.

Grab the 10 Key Questions you should have written in the Investor Q/A section of the book. Ask yourself each question in your mind, and then state your answer out loud. Once you've done that, you will probably find yourself tweaking your answers. Go through each question until each answer you have prepared sounds (and feels) right.

Step 2: Record yourself.

Record yourself answering each question out loud. Make any changes you feel are needed.

Step 3: Practice in front of people.

Gather some friends and family and give each them questions to ask during the presentation. Ask them to interrupt you in a natural way, once you've completed a thought. But let them choose when and where to do that and what questions to ask. Turn on your timer and record.

This is one of the most important skills to learn in an investor pitch, so if your friends and family are game, do this several times.

A Note About Technology

You have the killer presentation ready to go. You have practiced it and feel pretty confident. But you find that when you get to the investor's office, the WiFi doesn't work, the projector is down, or they would rather just have a printed copy of the slides and have you casually walk them through the presentation at their desk.

In most cases, you are going to have a very finite amount of time to speak with an investor, and the last thing you want to do is squander that dealing with technical difficulties. Bring several printed copies of your presentation with you and be prepared to go with the flow.

Now, if you have a very technical demo that requires you to show video or animation or even connect to the Internet, then have that prepared on your laptop. If it's a small group of people, this should be fine. If it's a large room and you feel you are doing your pitch a disservice and cannot deliver that killer presentation, ask if you can reschedule.

Assume that you won't be able to connect to the office projector or even connect to your website. Have a local copy of the website and application on your laptop and, if the Internet doesn't work, you'll be able to fire up your app without connecting to the network.

Also be ready to pitch without your deck. In some cases, you won't have access to a projector or the investors don't want to see your deck and instead want you to "talk." Be ready to offer a completely deck-free pitch when necessary.

TechCrunch Disrupt is the biggest and arguably most important startup event in the world. Dozens of startups take to the Disrupt stage in Startup Battlefield where they talk about their mission, their business, and their technology. And every single one of those startups began with a pitch that wouldn't have gotten them $5 let alone $500,000.

Although startup founders often understand implicitly the value of a good story, many of them fail to pitch investors with those stories. Say the company makes baby monitors. These monitors could be cheaper, better, and clearer than competitors' models. They could look cooler, last longer, and even lull the baby to sleep with synthetic noise. But putting all that on a deck makes the baby monitor seem more like an alien object than something you would trust to put in your baby's room. The answer, then, is a story.

Say the founder, Jane, had a young baby and she was constantly and needlessly worried. She bought the normal baby monitors and installed them, but each one failed spectacularly. One ran out of battery during movie night, and the baby was left crying for an hour. Another gave a false alert that suggested the baby wasn't breathing. Still another was hijacked by kids who had a basic walkie talkie, and they were making weird noises into the baby monitor. All of these stories add up to something new parents understand implicitly and respond to emotionally.

Then Jane talks about her journey. She connected with an old friend who went to MIT. She and her husband sold a sports car to build the first prototypes. They made the first models to look like a toucan so the baby would have something colorful to see. "After all," says Jane. "You want a baby monitor that will make your little one laugh."

All of this results in a narrative that anyone with a brain and a heart can follow. If Jane had talked about milliamp hours and the security systems built into the monitor the audience would fall asleep. If she describes an amazing new baby monitor that any new mom would love to own, then you get a different feeling and different energy.

The deck has to match that energy. Maybe there is one page in the appendix that features the speeds and feeds for the new monitor. But the first few pages of the deck should relate the story to the viewer. Every time we speak to a founder, we ask for a story. What caused this idea? What was lifelike before the idea became real? What does the world look like after everyone accepts the idea? This story – the hero's journey, if you will – is integral to any startup's pitch.

How to give a demo

There are many methods you can use to give a demo in a pitch meeting. But if you are going to do a demo that requires a lot of technical things to go right, you'd better have a backup plan.

Preparing a video of your demo ahead of time means you will always have it ready to go. Embed it in the presentation in case the live demo fails.

If you're building an app, use screenshots. In this scenario, as the app isn't finalized, this is the best, safest, and most engaging way to showcase the product. If you had a restaurant, this could be a menu, photos of food, or a rendering of the future restaurant space.

Nothing will ever beat a live demo. If you have a final product or a working prototype (you trust), make sure to practice giving this 1 to 2 -minute demo over and over before bringing it to an investor meeting.

Ready to pitch? Not so fast. Record yourself pitching and be prepared for some of the most grueling effort you're going to have to put into this process: watching yourself on screen.

Want to know the easiest and most fun way to pass out your deck to the public? Make a video of you presenting the deck. Shorten the deck a bit and focus on only the most important parts. Imagine you're talking to a potential customer in that video - not an investor - and you'll have a better chance of telling your story to an absolutely random person on the internet.

Core Presentation Skills

Begin this process by recording your pitch. Record yourself standing up wearing the clothes in which you'll normally be pitching. Don't wear a suit if you don't normally like to wear one nor should you wear dirty sweats. Make yourself comfortable but presentable.

Perform your pitch. If you mess up, start over from the top. Keep performing the pitch until it flows like butter.

Now that you've recorded a good version, watch the video. See if you can spot any of the following:

Did you seem stiff?

Did you wave your arms and hands around too much?

Did you use a lot of filler words and sounds like "um," "ahh" or "you know"?

Did you make eye contact with people in the room?

Did you speak for long periods of time, without taking a breath?

Avoid Filler Words and Sounds

We have all seen speakers who can't stop saying "um," "ahhh," "like," or "well" during a presentation. It's not only super distracting, it also makes the speaker seem unprepared. Why do we use filler words? It's a natural defense mechanism and gives our mind time to search for the right words or answers to questions. As you watch the video, note which filler words you use.

Recognize not only the filler words you use but when you are using them. Ask yourself, were you nervous, unprepared? Did it happen during the presentation or mainly when you were answering questions? If nervous, then it should have gotten better as you went along. If unprepared, then perhaps you need to practice your presentation and Q&A some more.

As you go through your day speaking to people, every time you notice yourself using a filler word, give your leg a tap. As you become aware of when and where you are using them, you will start catching yourself before they come out of your mouth. When you do, take a breath, pause, and then continue speaking without the filler word.

Practice in front of your friends and family. When you find yourself about to use a filler word, pause and make eye contact with someone for a brief moment. You may find that looking into someone's eyes makes it much harder to use filler words.

Keep it up. Once you are aware of filler words, you can over time work to eliminate them.

Eye Contact

Eye contact is part of everyday communication and in a presentation is a critical way to "check in" with the people in the room to make sure they are listening and taking in what you are saying. Eye contact also makes people feel more connected with a speaker. When you practice your speech with friends and family, make sure to shift your focus around the room and not fixate on one person. If you stay too long on one person this can have the opposite effect and make them uncomfortable. Make sure everyone in the room gets a few seconds of eye contact from time to time.

Dramatic Pauses

Combining eye contact and pauses when you speak is one of the most powerful tools in connecting with your audience. You should use pauses to 1) make sure you are speaking slowly   enough for the audience to take in what you are saying, 2) to make a point when something is really important and 3) to give people time to reflect on what you have just said.

Go through your presentation notes and add written PAUSE marks where you think they belong. Then, try practicing using these techniques. Record and also re-time your presentation to see if you are still coming in at 20 minutes. Chances are you may need to cut back on some words again when adding pauses.

Body Language

While practicing in front of your friends or family, you have probably noticed how you suddenly don't know what to do with your hands. Like filler words, when speaking publicly, our hands express our nervousness. Watch other presenters on stage to see what techniques others are using, then borrow what you like. You will develop your own technique over time, but as the saying goes, fake it until you make it.

Public Speaking vs. Pitching.

If you are going to speak on stage or in a large room filled with a lot of people, you should always stand. This puts you in a position of power and gives you the ability to see everyone. Make periodic eye contact with everyone in the room

However, if it is just you, a few people on your team, and one or two investors, it is more likely that you will be sitting when you pitch your deck. These meetings should be more conversational.

Tips when standing:

1. Stand up straight.

2. Never cross your arms or put your hands in your pockets.

3. When you don't know what to do with your hands, put them in a steeple, meaning have the tips of the fingers meet at your chest. Don't wave your arms around needlessly.

4. Keep your hands either in a neutral position by your side, with palms open, or in the classic steeple position when you don't need them.

5. Use your hands like a verb or an adjective – meaning don't use them all the time, but only when you really want to emphasize a point.

6. Move around. Don't stand in one place too long. Time your movement to new thoughts or transitions in your presentation.

7. Start your presentation with a smile, but don't smile

the whole time. Keep your face supple, not stiff.

8. Look around the room and make eye contact. Never stare too long, that will make people uncomfortable. Just a heartbeat.

Tips when sitting:

1. Sit up straight but lean in slightly to convey interest and engagement.

2. When you aren't using your hands, keep your wrists on the table (never your elbows).

3. Be animated. Use your face and voice to keep the investors' interest.

4. Take control. This is your meeting. Don't let people fidget. If they do, single them out for special interest, and remember to ask the other person pitching with you to watch out for problems. You will use these later when you discuss how the pitch went.

These tips aren't the end. You get better at public speaking with practice so you should be ready to pitch anytime and anywhere. Why not re-record your pitch a few months after you begin? Having trouble closing? Running the pitch again could give you the information you need to understand why your pitch is falling flat. A pitch is constantly changing and you should be ready to change with it.

Good Luck

Pitching is hard. Pitching is repetitive. Pitching is stressful. I've met founders who have gotten physically sick from the pitching process and some founders who gave up because it was too hard to get through to an investor who would listen.

The bottom line? Don't give up.

Your idea is important. Your idea is novel. Your idea is cool. You just have to package and pitch your idea in a way that will make everyone else agree with those three statements.

Again, don't get obsessed with giving the same pitch over and over again, ad infinitum. Know your target, know your goal, and know your pitch. Then, when possible, carefully target your pitch to each investor. Have fun with the pitch. Change things up when necessary and it's often a good idea to change up their pitch every few weeks in order to try new messages based on the things you've learned from previous pitches. Your pitch is not set in stone just as your business isn't stagnant (or at least it's not supposed to be.)

Here's the bottom line: you're building something. That's a great thing. Being a founder can be one of the most rewarding jobs on the planet, both financially and spiritually. It can also be a grind, a drag, and a death march. The instant that pitching becomes a chore is the instant you will fail.

Remember that you are doing something insanely difficult. Remember that you can get help. And remember that the rewards, when they come, will far outweigh the exhaustion you will feel pitching. This book is designed to give you the absolute best framework for a modern pitch and all you have to do is pour your heart and soul into the pitch to make it exactly what investors want to hear. Easy, huh?

In fact, it is. Only you know what your customers want. Only you know what your company is capable of. And only you know your product and market inside and out. Your pitch is the first offensive against investors and even global disinterest. Your pitch is a salvo against the investor's high, impenetrable walls. With the right mix, you just might crack that wall and make your investor crack a smile. And that, in the end, is often all it takes to turn your pitch into a check.